Pagan Portals

Chaos Magic

A Complete Beginner's Guide

What People Are Saying About

Chaos Magic

Chaos Magick is a complicated topic, yet in this short book you will find a clear and thorough explanation of its core axioms and concepts. Ivy Corvus is on the cutting edge of Chaos Magick forging a path that is as unique as it is true to the original version of the founders of our tradition. Chaos Magick is unlike any other branch of metaphysics, rather than telling you what to believe, Chaos Magick tells you why and how to believe. It replaces "woo woo" and overly complicated rituals with rational thought and experimentation. Ivy does this masterfully. If you want a no-nonsense approach to Magick and its underlying mechanisms then this is the book for you.
Sanhre Daffowt, host of *The Order of Chaos* podcast

Ivy's book is exactly what new practitioners of chaos magic need. It's a clear and concise manual that breaks down the fundamentals necessary to understand chaos theory and its real-world practice. The exercises throughout the book help break down barriers in conditioned thinking and allow the reader to leave old dogma behind. I particularly love the varying methods of working with sigils and magical entities as it explores the psychological and spiritual models of application, allowing for an experimental craft. I've read multiple books on chaos magic, but Ivy's leaves me feeling like I have a much more transparent understanding of how to step into the shoes of a chaos magician.
Marshall WSL, author of *Cunning Words: A Grimoire of Tales and Magic*

Finally, a book for beginners that isn't full of fluff and common fodder while also cutting through the noise of unnecessary complexity. As someone new to chaos magic, I've often felt frustrated by the lack of beginner-friendly resources. Books like *Liber Null* and *Condensed Chaos* are considered staples, but they were written decades ago. While they are foundational, they can also feel intimidating for someone just starting out. What I've been searching for is a book that embodies the spirit of chaos magic – its flexibility, creativity, and emphasis on personal experimentation – while also breaking things down in a way that's accessible to a modern audience. This book is exactly that.

What makes this book a necessity for today's aspiring chaos magician is how it bridges the gap between classic chaos magic books and the modern chaos movement. It explains core concepts like belief-shifting, sigils, and gnosis in a way that's easy to understand without sacrificing depth or complexity. Most importantly, it's written with the beginner in mind, offering practical exercises, and relatable examples. For anyone looking to dive into chaos magic without feeling overwhelmed, this book is the perfect place to start.

Justin Bennett, creator of "The Witch of Enchantment" on YouTube

Pagan Portals

Chaos Magic

A Complete Beginner's Guide

Ivy Corvus

MOON BOOKS

London, UK

Washington, DC, USA

CollectiveInk

First published by Moon Books, 2026
Moon Books is an imprint of Collective Ink Ltd.,
Unit 11, Shepperton House, 89 Shepperton Road, London, N1 3DF
office@collectiveinkbooks.com
www.collectiveinkbooks.com
www.moon-books.net

For distributor details and how to order please visit the 'Ordering' section on our website.

ISBN: 978 1 80341 872 8
978 1 78535 229 4 (ebook)
Library of Congress Control Number: 2024951551

A CIP catalogue record for this book is available from the British Library.

Design: Lapiz Digital Services
Illustrated by Kay Savage

UK: Printed and bound by CPI Group (UK) Ltd, Croydon, CR0 4YY
US: Printed and bound by Thomson-Shore, 7300 West Joy Road, Dexter, MI 48130

Contents

This book is dedicated to Thoth.
Thank you for everything.

Introduction

I was thirteen when I decided I was going to write a book someday. A grungy preteen obsessed with world religions – I had not yet been exposed to the undoing of chaos magic. I had no idea how aligned my perspective was at the time until now.

It was six in the morning. I was standing in the bathroom applying a thick layer of eyeliner while my mom, on the opposite end of our mobile home, applied mascara to hers.

That morning I told her, "My book will be about how all religions are equally true and valid but also equally false."

She laughed and said something along the lines of, "I have no doubt that one day you will, sissy."

In a way, I was right. Though I would not consider this book to be my magnum opus, it is the beginning of a journey – one in which I complete the mission I set out for myself at thirteen.

A common complaint I hear from budding chaos magicians, or those interested in chaos magic theory, is the lack of beginner-friendly books that are both accessible *and* substantial enough to convey the essence of chaos magic. This may be due to the nature of the chaos magic movement, which encourages personal exploration over dogmatic instruction. However, I believe there can be a balance.

Written as a short guide, simplifying the complexities of chaos magic theory without diluting its essence, this book will help you dip your toe into the alchemy arcade of chaos magic theory. If you savor chaos magic on your tongue and find its flavor inviting, there are thirty-one other books I have recommended at the end to expand your mind. As someone prone to lengthy explanations, I continuously reminded myself while writing this book that this is not meant to be an exhaustive analysis of chaos magic. Instead, I aim to fill a gap by providing an accessible beginner's guide – an easy-to-understand introduction to the basics.

Not only did I want this book to be accessible, while still offering enough depth to explain chaos magic theory, I also wanted it to be free of rigid doctrines on how one should practice. This is the book I wish I had when I started my journey into chaos magic many years ago.

I do not proclaim that this should be the only book you read on chaos magic. I must also emphasize that you do not have to read any books at all to practice chaos magic. An integral part of this practice involves personal experimentation. I encourage you to become the mad scientist that you are capable of embodying – to express full creative freedom and create something that is true blasphemy.

Ten years from now, I may disagree with everything I have written in this book. That is the beauty of chaos magic.

PART I

THEORY

Chapter 1

What Is Chaos Magic?

In this book, you will notice that I use the spelling "magic" rather than "magick." This is a deliberate choice. Aleister Crowley popularized the term "magick" to distinguish occult magical practices from stage magic. This aimed to highlight a deeper, more esoteric nature to his work. At the time, this distinction was important as it helped clarify the spiritual aspect of occult practices – to separate them from the silly entertainment of stage magicians pulling rabbits out of hats and sawing their assistants in half.

However, I believe in modern times, such distinctions are less necessary and the terms may be used interchangeably. The term "magic" has evolved. My use of "magic" is not meant to dismiss or undermine Crowley's contributions; rather, it reflects the practical nature of chaos magic. Chaos magic values personal experience and practicality over any rigid adherence to terminology. Please know that both 'magick' and 'magic' are valid terms, and my choice reflects another key principle of chaos magic: the importance of personal gnosis and individual interpretation.

What Is Magic?

Before exposing you to the kaleidoscopic funhouse of chaos magic, I must further clarify what I mean by "magic." The occult use of this term differs from magic depicted in movies, television, fantasy novels, and video games. Magic, in this context, is a spiritual practice that harnesses the forces of the universe to bring about desired changes in the practitioner's life. Unlike the silly, and sometimes grandiose spells in fantasy movies that defy natural laws, real magic is deeply rooted in willpower, intention, and the manipulation of subtle energies. It is about understanding the relationship between macrocosm and microcosm.

Aleister Crowley defined magic as "the Science and Art of causing Change to occur in conformity with Will." I can't help but roll my eyes a bit as I write this – not because Crowley's definition isn't important, but because it is quoted so often. If the occult had a selection of premade welcome mats, this would be one of the standard options at your local metaphysical store. Magic is not about waving a wand and instantaneously transforming one's reality. It can be seen as aligning one's Will with natural and spiritual laws to create the reality one wishes to experience.

Dion Fortune, another influential occultist often quoted, described magic as "the art of causing changes in consciousness in accordance with will." This definition emphasizes a psychological dimension of magic. By altering one's state of consciousness, the practitioner is able to tap into different planes of existence to make changes in the material world. Fortune's perspective also implies that magic is as much about personal transformation as it is about external manifestations.

Anton LaVey believed that "Magic is like nature itself, and successful magicians know that it is impossible to command the forces of nature; one can only direct and assist them in doing their will." This suggests that true magic works in harmony with natural forces rather than seeking to dominate or command them outright.

Magic often involves entering altered states of consciousness and performing various esoteric rituals by utilizing symbolism and connecting to spiritual forces. That is a very broad and ambiguous statement but magic is as diverse as the practitioners themselves. Magic is subtle. It requires patience. Unlike the instantaneous and exaggerated effects of magic in film, true magic is a gradual, introspective process. The dual focus of internal and external transformation is essential as true transformation begins from within. By aligning your internal state with your external intentions, you can create long-lasting, sustainable, and meaningful change.

Magical practices can vary from ceremonial magic (highly structured rituals from systems like the Hermetic Order of the Golden Dawn, Thelema, Solomonic magic, or Wicca), to various forms of folk magic, witchcraft, Christian mysticism, alchemy, and more. Chaos magic is merely one flavor of magic. It swims in a simmering stew with other practices that make up a vast world of occultism.

What Is Chaos Magic?

Chaos magic is a philosophy and a postmodern magical practice that centers around using your own belief as a tool to manifest the things you desire. This will be discussed further in Chapter 2 as we explore subjective versus objective reality and what it means to practice belief shifting. Chaos magic is also pragmatic and results-based. A crude illustration of the chaos approach to magic is, "If it works, do it. If it doesn't, fuck it." Chaos magic doesn't bother with detailed ceremonial procedures as it is a big "screw you" to such formalities. This topic is nuanced as practitioners can partake in detailed ceremonial procedures so long as it aligns with their overall goal – but not because they are adhering to rigid dogma. This will be discussed further in Chapter 3 as we explore the avoidance of dogmatism and what it means to remove limiting beliefs.

It is important to note that chaos magic is not necessarily a magical tradition in its own right – meaning there are no set rules to follow. Instead, it is more of a philosophical perspective on how magic works. I suppose one could say there are specific techniques chaos magicians tend to adopt: gnosis, working with sigils, creating magical entities, incorporating pop culture magic, and so on. These themes will be explored in Chapters 4 through 7. Although these techniques are practiced by many chaos magicians today, these techniques are not intrinsically chaos magic.

A chaos magician is practicing chaos magic when they prescribe to chaos magic theory.

At the expense of sounding redundant, magical techniques (such as working with sigils and servitors) are not inherently chaos magic. Many occultists from varying spiritual traditions may work with sigils and servitors, but this does not mean they prescribe to chaos magic theory nor does it mean they are practicing chaos magic.

Well then, what is chaos magic theory? That is what we will explore from Chapters 1 through 4.

Models of Magic

For centuries, occultists have questioned the driving forces and laws behind magic and the paranormal. If a witch casts a spell, a psychic channels messages, and a ceremonial magician evokes spirits or communes with the divine, what constitutes that power? Some may already be familiar with various models of magic that attempt to explain these phenomena:

- The **spirit model** of magic suggests that the power of magic comes from spiritual beings or entities. Practitioners may work with spirits, gods, or other supernatural forces to achieve their desires. In this model, spirits are objectively real regardless of the practitioner's belief in their existence.
- The **energy model** of magic suggests that the power of magic comes from energy. This model explains that there

are subtle, non-physical energies that exist and can be manipulated to bring about change in the physical or spiritual realms.

- The **psychological model** suggests that the power of magic comes from the practitioner's mind. By combining ritual, symbolism, and belief, the practitioner can affect their psyche and perception, causing physical changes in the external environment. Rather than believing in spirits, the practitioner working from the psychological model believes in projections of the subconscious mind.
- The **meta-model** of magic suggests that the power of magic is unknowable as we can only experience reality subjectively. Therefore, those who prescribe to the meta-model may use any other model of magic at any time as they see fit.

There are many other perspectives and models of magic that exist to explain how magic and paranormal phenomena occur. Chaos magic is sometimes placed under the psychological model of magic. However, I would argue that chaos magic adopts the meta-model of magic through belief shifting which will be discussed further in Chapter 2.

Chaos Magic Does Not Mean Disorganized Magic

Perhaps one of the biggest misunderstandings about chaos magic that I see is:

> "If an individual is chaotic and disorganized within their magical practice, they must be practicing chaos magic."

This is false. Chaos magic is not synonymous with a practice that is chaotic in the sense of disorganization. If one chooses to have a chaotic approach to their magic, that does not necessarily mean they prescribe to chaos magic theory. Chaos magic theory is what will be explored throughout the rest of this book. It encompasses using belief as a tool, belief shifting, the avoidance of dogmatism, deconstructing one's ego by removing limiting beliefs, achieving gnosis, and much more.

The term "chaos magic" can be somewhat misleading. The name derives not from the idea of disorder, but from the concept of chaos as a fundamental, creative force in the universe. In the context of chaos magic, "chaos" refers to the underlying unpredictable nature of reality which can be influenced by the magician's will and belief.

A Brief History

Austin Osman Spare, an English artist and occultist, is often credited as the grandfather of chaos magic. From the early to mid-1900s, Spare's work with sigils brought a unique perspective to the occult scene. At the time, western occultism was dominated by highly ritualized ceremonial magic – secret orders with strict dogma and ceremonial magic rituals performed from ancient grimoires. Spare's work with sigilization, the creation of his Alphabet of Desire, and his philosophical underpinnings showed the occult community that the "ceremonial" part of magic was entirely optional – one could achieve the same results without all the pomp and circumstance through art and personal gnosis. There was no need to go through long, arduous ceremonial magic rituals because one could simply create an image, implant that image into the subconscious mind, and manifest their desires subconsciously as they continue throughout their day. Spare's work, along with other occultists such as Kenneth Grant and Aleister Crowley, influenced the Western occult scene by introducing radical ideas that encouraged creativity, eclecticism, personal exploration, and experimentation.

By the 1970s, radical ideas pervaded the community. Peter J. Carroll, often credited as the official founder of chaos magic, published a book titled *Liber Null* in 1978 followed by a companion book, *Psychonaut* in 1982. In 1987, these books were combined into a single volume, *Liber Null & Psychonaut,* and still serve as a foundational text for the chaos magic movement today. Alongside Carroll, Ray Sherwin is considered a co-founder of chaos magic. He contributed to the development of chaos magic through his work *The Book of Results* published in 1978.

In *Condensed Chaos*, Phil Hine draws a parallel between chaos magic and punk subculture. When chaos magic was emerging in the 1970s and early 1980s, it coincided with the rise of punk. Both chaos magic and the punk subculture rejected traditional authority and sought to challenge societal norms. Both had themes of iconoclasm by rejecting established symbols and beliefs in favor of creating new ones. Hine's book *Condensed Chaos,* written in 1995, serves as another foundational text that expands upon Peter Carroll's radical ideas. Hine's book outlines what he identified as the six key principles of chaos magic: the avoidance of dogmatism, personal experience, technical excellence, deconditioning, diverse approaches, and gnosis.

Since then, chaos magic has continued to evolve.

Become a Mad Scientist

In an attempt to throw you into the fire of chaos magic, I'd like to introduce the concept of becoming your own magical scientist. Consider consecrating and bringing to life a magical journal that also serves as a spiritual entity to commune with. Your magical journal may contain the following:

- **Experiments:** Spells and rituals you have performed including the intention of the ritual, the date, ingredients, ritual tools used, any notable planetary alignments or timing, as well as the procedure performed.
- **Experiences:** Your personal experiences during the ritual including emotional states, visions, intuitive breakthroughs, and thoughts after completion.

- **Outcome documentation:** The results of your spells and/or rituals that detail how long it took to achieve a result, how closely it matched the intention, any errors that could be mitigated in the future, and lessons learned.
- **Dreams & Meditations:** Any dreams that seem significant or related to your spiritual work, messages received in meditations, detailed accounts of trips into the astral realm.
- **Symbols:** Sigils or a secret language you have created for yourself.
- **Research notes:** Any information from books, articles, and other resources pertinent to the study of your magic.
- **Invocations and evocations:** Chants and any script used to call upon spirits, gods, or entities.

Exercise 1: Bring Your Journal to Life

Imagine a journal that is not just a collection of blank pages but a living, breathing entity, a trusted companion on your magical journey. This journal is a sacred vessel for your thoughts, experiments, and intuitive messages. Consider giving your chaos magic journal a name. For the sake of this exercise, we will call her Alice.

This exercise takes you through consecrating and awakening your journal. By consecrating your journal, you are imbuing it with the beginnings of a spiritual entity. This only needs to be performed once upon establishing the journal's spirit. To awaken your journal, you will create some sort of symbol or gesture to perform. Each time you open your journal, perform the reawakening ritual to ensure it remains a powerful, living entity that continues to evolve. As you write, you commune with its spirit. The journal gains strength the more you write.

Materials:

- A blank journal or notebook.
- A consecration oil (crafted specifically for this purpose, blend a carrier oil with a few drops of essential oils associated with consecration. Examples: frankincense and myrrh).
- Incense (the type does not matter as you will be using the smoke but for additional correspondence, choose an incense that correlates with purification. Examples: frankincense, myrrh, sandalwood, cedar, rosemary, or copal).
- A writing instrument.
- A quiet, undisturbed space.

Procedure:

1. Find a quiet space where you can perform this ritual undisturbed. Later on, we will discuss what a ritual space is. But for now, a quiet place will suffice.
2. Choose and burn the appropriate incense to purify the space. Pass the journal through the smoke to remove any residual energies unwanted for this ritual.
3. Give your journal a name. The name is a crucial step in the consecration process as it is part of the act of creation. You are giving an identity and a presence to this journal, and it becomes more than a collection of pages. When you name your journal, you acknowledge its role as a living entity and a vital part of your magical practice.
4. If you haven't already, prepare a small amount of consecration oil.
5. Hold the journal in your hands and close your eyes. Take a few deep breaths to center yourself. When you are ready, anoint the journal with the consecration oil you

have prepared while clearly stating your intention for this journal. For example:

"I consecrate this journal, Alice, to be my sacred space for recording my magical experiments and discoveries. May Alice become a reliable spirit of knowledge, wisdom, and spiritual transformation."

6. Decide on a symbol or a gesture that you can use to awaken your journal each time you use it. The symbol could be a pentacle, a personal sigil, the chaos magic star, or any other symbol that intuitively speaks to you. If you choose to perform a gesture instead, this could be a specific way of moving your hands such as hovering a hand over the journal, palm side up, and bringing your first and fifth digits together. Whatever the symbol or gesture, it is important to remain consistent. For this first initial awakening, dip your finger into the consecration oil and trace the chosen symbol over the cover of the journal. If you have created a gesture instead, anoint your hands with consecration oil prior to performing the gesture. State your intentions clearly as you do this:

   "Awaken, Alice, and guide my hand in the pursuit of knowledge."

7. Complete this ritual with a final blessing. Pick up the journal and state what intuitively comes to mind. You may choose to say something akin to:

   "May you become a loyal companion on my magical journey. Together, we will grow in power. As I write within these pages, may my magic grow stronger."

8. After this ritual is complete, continue to use the journal in subsequent days simply by tracing the awakening symbol or performing the awakening gesture over the book prior to opening the journal. The consecration oil only needs to be used once but feel free to modify this ritual as you see fit. The most important part of any chaos magic ritual is to *do what works*.

As there are no rules and no limitations within a chaos magic practice, I can merely provide you with the inspiration to create your own practice. A chaos magician is encouraged to experiment and find what techniques best suit their unique psyche. Take what resonates within this book, leave what doesn't, and know that themes discussed throughout this book may be viewed as general guidelines rather than strict rules to follow.

Chapter 2

Belief as a Tool

"Nothing is true, everything is permitted."

The origin of this phrase is obscure and many will be familiar with it from the *Assassin's Creed* video game. It is often incorrectly attributed to Friedrich Nietzsche, a German philosopher, and is rumored to originate from Hassan-i Sabbah – a military leader in the 11th century. Over the years, this expression has become somewhat of an unofficial slogan for chaos magic.

To say that "nothing is true" is to acknowledge that our human consciousness is unable to experience the world objectively. Our five physical senses are filtered through our individual experiences, biases, and interpretations. What one perceives may be different from what another perceives.

Each individual holds cognitive biases that affect the way information is processed and interpreted. These biases are often unconscious and can influence our decisions, judgments, and perceptions, leading to highly individualized experiences.

Not only do the five physical senses, our own personal biases, and our experiences shape the reality we experience, cultural and social factors play a huge role in shaping filters in our minds. Cultural norms and societal expectations influence how people perceive and interpret events, making objectivity even more of a challenge. Oftentimes, individuals within some sort of societal framework are influenced or even manipulated into adopting certain beliefs or behaviors that align with the ideologies of that society.

Subjective and objective reality represent two different ways of perceiving the world:

- **Objective reality** refers to the external, independent existence of things regardless of an individual's perception or interpretation.
- **Subjective reality** is based on personal opinions, feelings, perceptions, and interpretations.

The idea that a human can't have a completely objective experience stems from the inherent subjectivity of human perception and cognition.

An example that challenges the existence of true objectivity comes from quantum mechanics, specifically the double-slit experiment. In this experiment, particles like electrons are shown to behave both as particles and waves, depending on whether they are being observed. When not observed, they pass through both slits simultaneously, existing in a state of probability. But the moment they are observed, they "choose" a specific path and act like particles. This phenomenon suggests that reality at its fundamental level is shaped by the act of observation itself. Even the mere act of perceiving something alters reality, demonstrating that there is no fixed, objective reality independent of observation. If reality shifts based on whether or not it is being observed, then our belief in an objective universe dissolves. What we perceive as reality might be nothing more than an illusion, a projection shaped by our consciousness, where nothing exists in a fixed state. This will be discussed further in Chapter 4.

Chaos magic theory aligns with this and argues that it is impossible to identify any true objective reality. Because our experience of reality is subjective, one cannot claim that gods, spirits, or any moral facts are objectively real. If one feeds their belief into the idea of a god or a spirit being real, then that god or spirit becomes real in that person's experience. However, if the individual were to cease believing in the existence of a god or spirit, it would cease to have any sort of power or influence over the individual's life – thus no longer existing in that person's version of reality.

Of course, humans can strive to be as objective as possible. In fact, a regular practice of self-awareness, critical thinking, and impartial decision-making is important and can allow us to bypass certain cognitive biases. However, complete objectivity, free from all personal influences, is a quixotic ideal.

Chaos magic argues that we cannot detach completely from our human experience to be able to claim that any sort of objective reality is true. This not only includes the existence of gods and spirits, but any sort of framework that claims to hold universal truth. I would argue that this does not suggest that an objective reality cannot exist; rather, we can't claim any one particular *version* of reality to be true.

To say that "everything is permitted" is to acknowledge that because nothing is true, and there is no objective reality that can be observed from our human experience, we have full creative freedom to create the reality we desire. If one believes in a God or spirit and uses that spiritual power to manifest their desires into the material realm, then it is their *belief* in God or spirit that gives the magical working its power. It does not matter whether God or spirits are objectively true. What matters is the chaos magician's belief.

Blind Men and the Elephant

To further illustrate the idea of subjective reality, there is an old fable known as the "Blind Men and the Elephant" that has been used in various religious and spiritual traditions such as Buddhism and Hinduism. This fable tells the story of six blind men who encounter an elephant for the first time. As they attempt to understand what the elephant is, they find that they cannot agree.

The first blind man touches the side of the elephant and concludes it is like a wall. The second blind man touches the trunk of the elephant and concludes it is like a snake. The third blind man touches the leg of the elephant and concludes it is like a tree. The fourth blind man touches a tusk of the elephant and concludes it is like a spear. The fifth blind man touches an ear of the elephant and concludes it is like a fan. The sixth and final blind man touches the tail of the elephant and concludes it is like a rope.

Each blind man perceives only a small part of the elephant leading them to vastly different conclusions. The blind men argue and insist that their perspective is the one that is true. This fable demonstrates how perception can be subjective and limited. We can argue amongst ourselves whether one true god exists, multiple gods exist, no god exists, or whether god is not necessarily a man sitting in the clouds but rather a type of energy that is interspersed within everything here on this earth. Whatever our belief, we cannot claim it to be the ultimate truth as we are merely blind men tracing the features of an elephant.

Another point that this fable makes is though the blind men are unable to grasp what the elephant truly is due to their subjective experiences, there *is* some sort of objective reality present (the elephant). Though we do not have the means of understanding the bigger picture, the elephant in this fable does exist. I would argue that the elephant only exists in this timeline, in this moment, in this dimension of reality.

What truly matters from the chaos magic perspective is that we have the power to manipulate and create the reality we wish to experience by choosing what we feed our belief into. With this framework, you are using your belief as a tool to manifest the things you desire. Whether spirits objectively exist or not does not matter. Whether gods exist or not does not matter. Whether magic comes from the manipulation of small energy particles or whether it comes from the manipulation of one's subconscious mind, *it does not matter*. Arguing whether something is objectively real is irrelevant so long as working with these things brings subsequent results to the magician.

Belief Shifting

Now that we have established the use of belief as a tool, let's explore the technique of "belief shifting," also known as "paradigm jumping." Belief shifting is the process of intentionally adopting and discarding beliefs as they suit the magical practitioner.

In the early days of chaos magic it was argued that magic could be understood through the psychological model, where the practitioner's mind is the source of magical power. By shifting one's belief, the magician is able to tap into different parts of their psyche to manifest their desires. This idea aligns with the tendency of many chaos magicians (or "chaotes" for short) to lean towards atheism or agnosticism as the power resides in the magician's mind.

However, as I mentioned in Chapter 1, chaos magic can also be viewed through the meta-model, which suggests that the true nature of magical power is unknowable. This model allows practitioners to adopt any belief system temporarily to achieve their desired outcomes.

For instance, if a magician chooses to believe in gods or spirits for a ritual, they would fully immerse themselves in that belief, effectively using the spirit model.

This flexibility can be controversial, especially given chaos magic's origins in atheism and the rejection of religious dogma. However, as we will discuss in Chapter 3, chaos magic also rejects the dogma of chaos magic. The avoidance of dogmatism can be interpreted as the rejection of religious *and* atheistic dogma, embracing flexibility and adaptability in belief.

Here, I have introduced a chaos magic conundrum – a conundrum in which you, the budding chaote, can draw your own interpretation. To keep things simple: regardless of what you may be doing in your chaos practice, if you believe that it is your *belief* powering the magical working, you are prescribing to a piece of chaos magic theory.

Exercise 2: Belief Shifting with Dice

This exercise is a slightly modified and expanded version of the dice exercise found in *Liber Null* by Peter Carroll. Carroll suggests using a six-sided die to determine what beliefs to adopt as a way of breaking down habitual patterns and invoking chaos into the magician's life.

Materials:

- One six-sided die.
- Your magical journal.
- A writing instrument.

Procedure:

- In your magical journal, write down which side of the die corresponds to which belief system:
  1. Monotheism
  2. Polytheism
  3. Pantheism
  4. Animism
  5. Atheism
  6. Agnosticism

- Roll the six-sided die to determine which belief system you will adopt first.
- For at least one week, but preferably a full month, attempt to view life through the lens of the assigned belief system. Try to genuinely adopt the belief system's worldview and interpret situations and experiences as someone who fully embraces that paradigm.
- During this time, research the chosen belief system to understand its core tenets, rituals, practices, and perspectives. Engage in activities or rituals that are part of that belief system to deepen your immersion.
- Throughout the week or month, journal your experiences, thoughts, and feelings in your magical journal. Reflect on the following:

    1. How does this belief system influence your perception of daily events?
    2. What challenges or resistance do you encounter while trying to adopt this belief?
    3. What insights or new understandings do you gain from this experience?

- Once you have completed the assigned period for the first belief system, roll the die again to select the next belief system to adopt. Repeat the process until you have experienced all six belief systems.
- After completing the exercise with all six belief systems, write a final reflection in your journal. Compare and contrast your experiences with each belief. Reflect on how this exercise has impacted you overall.

The purpose of this exercise is to push yourself out of your comfort zone and explore new perspectives. By challenging your habitual ways of thinking and experiencing the world, you open yourself up to new insights and growth. This exercise is meant to challenge you, to invoke discomfort and uncertainty, and to encourage the development of new neural pathways.

To take this a step further, one could create a list consisting of six different actions or behaviors one could perform. The idea is to introduce ideas that are bizarre, nonsensical, radical, and contradictory to ideas the magician typically subscribes to. Next, the practitioner would assign each action a number from one to six. The practitioner would then roll the six-sided die and perform the corresponding action or behavior.

Some examples of different actions or behaviors could be:

- Speaking in riddles for an entire day
- Creating art blindfolded
- Writing a love letter to an inanimate object
- Adopting an opposite personality trait
- Inventing a ceremonial ritual for a mundane task
- Mimicking an animal for an hour
- Inventing a new language and using it
- Mapping a world that doesn't exist

This exercise is meant to introduce randomness and unpredictability, challenging the practitioner to break free from routine. This exercise also prepares the magician to "fake it until they make it" and introduces playfulness into a chaos magic practice.

Chapter 3

Deconditioning

In the previous chapter, I discussed what it means to use your belief as a primary tool for manifesting the reality you desire. Your belief in something makes it real. I also introduced the concept of belief shifting, or paradigm jumping, when magicians intentionally adopt and discard beliefs at will. A question I hear often is, "Why?" Why would a chaote go through a process of belief shifting, what does it look like, and how often does this truly happen? What is the importance of shifting one's belief?

Paradigm Jumping & the Psyche

The first reason is that paradigm jumping allows the chaote to tap into different aspects of their psyche. Our minds are complex with rainbows of layers that are often in conflict or contradiction with one another. Each belief system, or paradigm, resonates with different parts of the psyche. Paradigm jumping allows the chaote to operate from the psychological model of magic and manipulate reality to what they wish to see and experience.

For example, adopting a belief in a pantheon of deities might unlock archetypal energies within the magician. This gives access to symbols deeply embedded in the unconscious mind. By consciously moving between various paradigms, the chaote learns to see the world from multiple perspectives, broadening their understanding of reality and therefore enhancing their ability to shape it.

Pragmatism & Results

The second reason is that chaos magic is extremely pragmatic and results-based. One of the core tenets of chaos magic (though the use of the word 'tenet' is a loose one) is finding the most efficient way for the magician to get what they want. Chaos magic rejects limiting dogma and wants to get straight to the point: what works and what doesn't? By paradigm jumping, the chaote can immerse themselves in a belief for a short duration, achieve what they want, then shift their perspective to something else.

Not all magic may be practical for any given situation. For example, one situation may call for a witch's candle spell (let's say where you are temporarily subscribing to the energy model), whereas another situation may be more effectively handled by petitioning a saint (where you are temporarily subscribing to the spirit model).

This is a simplified example and there is more nuance to this conversation. For example, a witch casting a candle spell does not always subscribe to the energy model. Also, subscribing to the spirit model comes with respecting the spirits you work with and truly believing in their existence. The magician maintains this belief for the total duration they operate from this model. Later in this chapter, I will discuss how long a chaote can actually spend sitting in one particular belief system. I am merely trying to convey what it looks like when jumping paradigms. Belief shifting allows the chaote to experiment, try new things, and determine which techniques work best for their psyche. Being able to experiment and figure out what works best allows the practitioner to streamline their practice so that it is practical, efficient, and results-based.

Personal Gnosis & Psychological Deconstruction

This last reason comes from my personal gnosis (which, again, is an integral part of any chaos magic practice). Frequent and successful paradigm jumping leads to a deconstruction of the practitioner's psyche.

When I began to regularly practice belief shifting, something happened to my brain. I still, to this day, cannot quite articulate it to someone who has not experienced this. Frequent belief shifting broke down barriers in my mind I never knew existed.

When I began my journey with chaos magic, truly investing in practices such as the dice exercise outlined in Chapter 2 and my own experimentations, something unexpected happened. At first, it was incredibly difficult to shift my mindset. As an atheist for many years who desperately wanted to believe in spirits (like I did as a child), I had tried and failed. I performed various ceremonies to evoke spirits with no success. My mind had been conditioned to believe that spirits could not exist and as a result, I was not able to experience them. I always found myself jealous of those who could easily experience paranormal activity. After shifting my perspective from the idea of ultimate truths (atheism being the ultimate truth exemplified here) I was able to remove blockages and limitations that had held me captive for so long.

Now, I am not saying that the existence of spirits is objectively true. I personally subscribe to the belief that gods and spirits can both exist and not exist depending on the dimension of reality one is operating from. For those curious and wanting further elaboration, I will direct you to an essay I wrote in *This is Chaos*; a chaos magic anthology edited by Peter J. Carroll. This philosophical discussion is a distraction from the topic at hand.

To summarize: after successful paradigm jumping for many years, I no longer need to follow strict, regimented belief-shifting techniques to get myself to believe in something new. It became easier with time and practice to adopt new beliefs. However, for a beginner, a strict and regimented approach may be necessary. I encourage you to have patience and persistence with any stubborn, long-held beliefs you may hold. It can be difficult at first to decondition one's mind but the process is well worth the effort. If you can shed limiting beliefs, your potential to become more effective in your practice increases.

To illustrate this, let's consider another scenario: you were indoctrinated by a religious cult as a child or young adult. At the time, you may not realize how religious indoctrination imposes limiting beliefs on your psyche. If you were to leave this cult, you might no longer align with those beliefs. Yet, you may still experience lingering effects from the conditioning you experienced such as guilt or shame. These are limitations imposed on the psyche. These limitations are just as damaging (if not more) than a scenario like mine: an atheist who desperately wanted to experience spirits again but struggled to push past the rationality imposed by society. These examples show how one can be influenced by limiting beliefs and how difficult it can be to identify and remove them.

Shedding limiting beliefs is necessary and it allows you to experience personal growth. Limiting beliefs can also act as barriers to manifesting the things you want. By releasing these limiting beliefs, you attract more of what you truly desire.

Deconstructing Ego

To further remove stubborn and limiting beliefs, one may undergo a process of deconstructing their ego. Though "ego" can be defined in many ways depending on the culture and spiritual tradition, the ego can be seen as the part of yourself that deals with identity, self-image, and the conscious sense of "I" or "me". It encompasses beliefs, desires, fears, and the stories we tell ourselves about who we are. Our ego helps us navigate this world, but it also imposes limitations and filters our experiences through a lens of conditioning and societal expectations.

In the psychological model of magic, the ego is seen as both a tool and an obstacle. It can be a tool as it helps focus intention and direct magical operations. However, it is also an obstacle due to its attachment to rigid beliefs and self-concepts can limit the magician's ability to explore new paradigms. Deconstructing the ego through chaos magic practices allows the magician to access deeper layers of the psyche, free from the constraints of egoic identity. I like to envision the balance of a healthy ego and the higher, more enlightened self as a dance within the psyche. The exercise below is designed to help you begin the process of assessing and deconstructing your ego.

Exercise 3: Subconscious Belief Journaling

You may recognize these journaling prompts from my essay in *This is Chaos*. I must include them here. When belief shifting is performed, we are not only working with the conscious mind but also the subconscious which often holds beliefs we are not aware of. These beliefs can include self-sabotaging behaviors and thought patterns such as:

- I do not have the power to change my reality.
- I fear change; it makes me uncomfortable.
- This is all childish make-believe.

It is necessary to deconstruct these beliefs so they do not influence the effectiveness of your magic. Take out your magical journal and write about any limiting beliefs or thought patterns you wish to change. Start a regular journaling practice that involves the following prompts:

- Where did these limiting beliefs come from?
- What past experiences may have influenced these beliefs?
- What messages did you receive from authority figures or society about these beliefs? (Example: Is this really

childish make-believe or is that a belief imposed from the society or culture you grew up in?)

- What reoccurring patterns or themes do you notice in your life about this? Do you tend to dismiss similar beliefs?
- How do you talk to yourself internally?
- What fears or insecurities surface when you consider making these changes in your life?
- What would it mean to you and what would it look like if you let go of these limiting beliefs?

Limiting subconscious beliefs are why it is necessary to enter altered states of consciousness prior to performing any occult rituals. This will be discussed further in Chapter 4. When entering altered states of consciousness, the conscious mind is relinquishing control and the practitioner is better able to implant these new beliefs into the subconscious mind.

Ultimately, frequent and regular belief shifting can result in a deconstruction of the mind by removing limiting beliefs, assessing one's ego, and building new connections. Transmutation of the mind is part of one's Great Work and can lead to the discovery of one's True Will.

The Great Work, True Will & Chaos Magic

The Great Work is a term used in many esoteric traditions, such as Hermeticism and Alchemy, to describe the process of spiritual growth, enlightenment, and self-realization. In chaos magic, this process is about the transformation of the self through continuous experimentation and adaptation. The Great Work involves deconstructing and reconstructing one's beliefs and paradigms, ultimately aiming to discover and align with one's True Will.

True Will is a concept originating from Aleister Crowley referring to a person's ultimate purpose or destiny. It is the highest expression of an individual's unique nature and potential, free from societal expectations and personal illusions.

The practice of belief shifting in chaos magic can be seen as more than merely adopting different paradigms for practical outcomes. It is a spiritual exercise that contributes to one's Great Work by deconstructing and reconstructing the psyche and aligning the practitioner with their True Will. Through this process, the chaos magician achieves a deeper understanding of themselves ultimately leading to spiritual growth and self-realization. It is important to note that the philosophy of chaos magic does not innately prescribe to any rules or dogma. This perspective on belief shifting may be practiced by some magicians, but not all. The most important thing to remember is: *do what works.*

Belief Shifting Durations

How often does a chaote practice belief shifting and for how long do they stay in any particular paradigm? The duration of belief shifting varies greatly among chaos magicians and it depends on the individual goals of the practitioner. Some chaotes might adopt a new belief system for a short period, such as a few days or weeks, to achieve a specific magical goal. Others might immerse themselves in a paradigm for months or even years to deeply explore its impact on their psyche.

A chaote remains in a belief system as long as it is useful, meaningful, and productive. Once the belief system no longer serves these purposes, the chaote moves on, seeking new paradigms that better align with their objectives. This ensures that the practitioner continuously adapts and grows, avoiding stagnation and dogmatic thinking. A regular practice of reflection and journaling is crucial for this process as the chaote is encouraged to document their experiences, successes, challenges, and transformation.

I have come across this question from students in various forms: "What if I want to work with Hecate for the rest of my life? Can I still be a chaote?" My first response to this question is: I am not qualified, nor is anyone else qualified, to determine whether you are or are not a chaote. But to provide a more direct answer: if it works, it works. *A chaote may remain in any belief system as long as it is useful, meaningful, and productive.* As long as the chaote believes that it is their *belief* that gives Hecate power, they are still prescribing to chaos magic theory. However, if that belief were to become rigid adherence with an unwillingness to consider alternative viewpoints, then it is time to decondition one's mind. If the practitioner were to start believing that Hecate is objectively real, regardless of their belief in Hecate, then that would not typically be considered chaos magic. Remember, chaos magic theory rejects the idea of a definable objective reality and instead embraces chaos and the subjectivity of human perception.

Avoidance of Dogmatism

Finally, we have come to the avoidance of dogmatism. Dogmatism can be defined as the rigid adherence to a particular set of beliefs or doctrines, often accompanied by an unwillingness to consider alternative viewpoints even if opposing evidence is presented. Chaos magicians avoid dogmatism because it limits their ability to adapt, experiment, and evolve. Dogmatic thinking imposes constraints on the practitioner's creativity and freedom, which are essential components of chaos magic. Remember the conundrum I presented you with in Chapter 2? Chaos magic rejects limiting dogma including any limiting dogma that may be imposed by chaos magic itself.

Deconditioning, therefore, is not just about shedding old beliefs but also about cultivating the ability to move between beliefs with ease. It is a tool that enhances the chaote's ability to manipulate their own psyche, and through it, the fabric of their reality. A mind that is not bound by rigid beliefs is a mind that is free to explore, experiment, and create without the constraints of dogma or fixed perspectives.

When adopting a new belief system, it is important not to let that belief system become a new form of dogma. The purpose of belief shifting is to explore different paradigms, not to become confined by them. To avoid dogmatism, I encourage you, the budding chaote, to strive for a healthy balance between skepticism and open-mindedness. Be open to change and ready yourself to discard a belief system when it no longer brings results. The ability to let go of outdated and unproductive beliefs is a key component of chaos magic theory. By continuously questioning, adapting, and experimenting, chaotes ensure that their magical work remains creatively aligned with their evolving understanding of reality and self.

Exercise 4: The Mirror Mind

This ritual is designed to symbolically deconstruct limiting beliefs and ego, allowing the practitioner to embrace new paradigms. It is designed to be performed in conjunction with Exercise 3 as the introspection acquired through Exercise 3 is necessary for the effectiveness of this ritual.

To clarify a bit of terminology that will be used in this exercise and other exercises moving forward, there is a difference between *ritual* and one's *ritual space*. A ritual, in an occult sense, is a series of actions performed to produce a desired outcome. For instance, this could be invoking a spirit, engaging in spiritual devotion, or performing banishing and cleansing rituals to manage energies in a space or within yourself. Rituals can be performed for a myriad of intentions. Ritual space refers to the physical or mental area that has been prepared for the ritual to take place. I recommend finding a place where you can perform rituals – a place that you can make sacred. You may choose to set up an altar, cleanse the space physically and spiritually, light candles and incense, and visualize an energetic boundary encompassing the space where you, and you alone, can transcend the veil of the ordinary.

Materials:

- A hand mirror.
- A candle (preferably white or black).
- Your magical journal.
- A writing utensil.
- A small bowl of water.
- A small bowl of salt.

Procedure:

1. Set up your ritual space with the hand mirror, candle, bowls of water and salt, and your magical journal. Light the candle and place it in front of you.
2. Sit comfortably and take a few deep breaths, inhaling through your nose and exhaling through your mouth. Feel your body relaxing with each breath. Close your eyes and visualize roots extending from your body into the earth, grounding you and connecting you to the stabilizing energy of the earth.
3. Pick up the hand mirror and look into your own eyes as you reflect on any limiting beliefs or self-concepts you wish to deconstruct. Speak these beliefs aloud, acknowledging their presence and their impact on your life. Continuing with our examples from Exercise 3, these may include:

- "I do not have the power to change my reality."
- "I fear change."
- "This is all childish make-believe."

4. Dip your fingers into the bowl of water and sprinkle it over the mirror's surface. As you do this, visualize the water cleansing and purifying the mirror, washing away the limiting beliefs you have acknowledged.
5. Begin to focus on the flame of the candle. Visualize the glow of the flame growing brighter until it surrounds you, filling you completely. Hold the mirror up to the flame and gaze into the reflection of the flame. See this flame entering the mirror and transforming it into a tool of empowerment.
6. Take a pinch of salt and sprinkle it over the mirror. Salt plays a significant role not only as a physical purifying agent but also as a symbolic representation of mental alchemy. This concept is deeply rooted in the work of Carl Jung. Jung adopted symbolism to describe various mental processes. In his framework, "salts" of the mind refer to the crystallized, often rigid structures of thought and belief that shape our conscious experience. These salts can be both protective and limiting. In the context of this ritual, sprinkling salt over the mirror serves a dual purpose. Physically, it purifies the mirror, preparing it as a tool for introspection. Symbolically, it signifies the breaking down of these crystallized mental salts – fixed, limiting beliefs and self-concepts that no longer serve the practitioner. As you sprinkle the salt, say something akin to:

"With this salt, I cleanse away this limiting belief. I am open to new beliefs and possibilities."

7. Set the mirror aside and take up your magical journal. Write down the limiting beliefs you spoke aloud, and next to each one, write a new, empowering belief to replace it. For example:

    - "I do not have the power to change my reality" becomes "I have the power to create my reality."
    - "I fear change" becomes "I embrace change as a path to growth."
    - "This is all childish make-believe" becomes "This powerful practice unlocks my true potential."

8. Hold the mirror up to your face and say something akin to:

    "I see my true self, free from limitations. I am open to change and growth. I embrace the unknown."

9. Take a few moments to sit quietly, feeling the shift in your mindset and energy. When you feel ready, blow out the candle with confidence. Over the next few days, revisit your magical journal and read the new empowering beliefs you have written. Repeat this ritual daily, weekly, or monthly until limiting beliefs are replaced and you are confident in your ability to shape reality.

Chapter 4

Gnosis

Fair warning: this will be the most technical chapter in the book.

Altered states of consciousness are the key to ritual success. *Gnosis* typically refers to a deep sense of knowing or acquired personal wisdom particularly when it comes to spiritual truth. From the chaos magic perspective, gnosis refers to an altered state of consciousness (often called a "gnostic state") where the practitioner has shifted their consciousness to focus on a singular point or intention. This gnostic state allows the magician to quiet their mind – achieving a state of "no mind" – to focus on the goal of the ritual.

The process of entering an altered state allows the conscious (rational) mind to relinquish control, giving the practitioner greater access to their subconscious mind, the astral realm, and beyond. In order to create real change in the practitioner's life, one is advised to enter a gnostic state prior to performing any occult ritual. There are two main categories of altered states: inhibitory and excitatory.

Inhibitory States

Inhibitory states involve reducing sensory input and mental activity, allowing the practitioner to achieve a deep state of stillness. This can be achieved through mind-calming techniques such as:

- Meditative Trance: By meditating and becoming a silent observer of your mind, you can achieve a state of stillness. This can also be induced through visualization or other forms of meditation.
- Sensory Deprivation: Techniques such as sitting in complete darkness or silence can help to reduce external stimuli. Sensory deprivation tanks can also help to facilitate a gnostic state.
- Breathwork: Practices like pranayama or other forms of breathwork can slow the mind and bring the practitioner in tune with their body.
- Exhaustion: This is achieved through sleep deprivation, fasting, or intense physical exertion and can push the mind and body into an altered state. However, it is not recommended unless you are knowledgeable about how to execute this safely without harming your health.
- Death Posture: Developed by Austin Osman Spare, this technique involves a specific physical posture combined with intense concentration, leading to a state of complete mental and physical stillness.
- Sound: Low chanting, monotonous drumming, or using mantras, tuning forks, singing bowls, binaural beats, and other slow, repetitive, rhythmic sounds can be used to calm the mind.
- Trance-Inducing Drugs: Some chaos magicians use hypnotic or psychoactive substances to achieve altered states. This method is controversial and carries significant risks, so it is not recommended unless approached with caution and thorough understanding.

Inhibitory states are particularly useful for introspective work, divination, traversing the astral realm, communicating with spirits, and any occult rituals that require a high degree of inner focus and stillness. By entering a state of stillness, the practitioner can bypass the conscious mind's interference, allowing for a deeper connection with the subconscious and the spiritual realm.

Excitatory States

Excitatory states involve stimulating the mind and body to the point of intense arousal and ecstasy. Excitatory states are characterized by heightened sensory input and increased activity – whether it be mental and/or physical. Activities to induce an excitatory state include:

- Physically Moving Your Body: Dancing, drumming, and other forms of rhythmic movement can bring the practitioner into ecstasy.
- Emotional Stimulation: Intense emotions (such as anger, fear, embarrassment, despair, joy, pleasure, and so on) can lead to an ecstatic frenzy. Many chaos magicians use laughter as a powerful tool to achieve an excitatory gnostic state.
- Sexual Excitation: Harnessing sexual energy through arousal or orgasm allows the practitioner to experience ecstasy and send powerful energy toward their magical intent.
- Sound: Loud and repetitive sounds such as chanting or singing can overwhelm the senses and induce an excitatory state. This differs from the low, slow, rhythmic sounds used for inhibitory states.
- Hyperventilation: This increases oxygen levels in the blood, creating a sense of euphoria.
- Excitatory Drugs: Similar to hypnotic drugs, some practitioners may use disinhibitory drugs, such as mild hallucinogens, to achieve excitatory states. Due to potential dangers and health risks, I cannot ethically endorse this approach.

Excitatory states are effective for rituals that require a burst of energy such as banishing a spirit, manifesting certain desires, and working within a group. When in an ecstatic state, the practitioner can harness this energy and direct it toward their magical intent.

Which One Do You Choose?

Certain rituals may inherently benefit from one type of gnostic state over the other. For instance, when performing divination (which involves receiving subtle messages from spiritual entities or the subconscious mind) an inhibitory state might be more beneficial. A still mind can better tune into subtle energies and symbols, providing clearer guidance and understanding of the reading. However, when you need to perform a banishing or protective ritual, an excitatory state could provide the necessary intensity to effectively clear negative energies out of your space and create a strong protective barrier.

In addition, there are many scenarios where it would be appropriate to use either approach: inhibitory or excitatory. For example, when we discuss the use of sigils in Chapter 5, either approach can be used to charge a sigil. Inhibitory states can help you focus intently on the sigil, embedding it deep into your subconscious mind. Excitatory states, on the other hand, can empower the sigil with a surge of energy, launching it into the astral realm with force. It is up to the chaote to experiment with different gnostic states and determine which technique works best for which ritual.

Meditative Trance States

Achieving a meditative trance is one of the most important techniques a practitioner can use to enter a gnostic state. Unlike other methods that involve less control, meditative trances allow the practitioner to maintain a high degree of mental clarity and intentionality. For executing rituals accurately and effectively, and for the ability to enter or exit the gnostic state at will, meditation is ideal. A meditative trance ensures that the practitioner remains focused on their magical intent without becoming overwhelmed by other sensations.

At the expense of providing a bit of personal bias here, (take it or leave it) meditation is the key to ritual success as it helps to bypass the conscious mind. The conscious mind is often called the "rational mind" because its primary job is to make sense of the world around you. Our brains receive constant external stimuli. The conscious mind takes these external stimuli and filters anything out that doesn't match or pass our reality threshold to weave a story that is logical and sensible.

A reality threshold is the point at which the brain decides what is real and what is not based on its internal model of the world. This filtering mechanism is important for navigating daily life, as it helps maintain a consistent and practical perception of reality. However, this same mechanism can become a barrier when attempting to access altered states of consciousness or the spirit realm, as it tends to dismiss or rationalize away any experiences that don't fit within our established framework of reality.

Research has shown that our brains are constantly filtering sensory information to create a coherent experience of reality. Research by neuroscientist Dr. Anil Seth suggests that perception is a controlled hallucination, where the brain makes predictions about sensory input and updates these predictions based on actual sensory data. This means that what we perceive as reality is, to some degree, a constructed experience shaped by our brain's predictions and interpretations.

The conscious mind can also be called the "critical" mind. Overly analytical thinkers will resonate with what I'm about to say here: it is often incredibly difficult to perform occult rituals, talk to spirits, or engage in anything paranormal without feeling silly or as if it's all childish fantasy. The critical mind is always looking for logical explanations and tends to dismiss anything that doesn't fit within its rational framework.

To perform occult rituals with stronger belief, one must bypass the critical conscious mind. To do this, the practitioner can enter a meditative trance. This is when the conscious mind relinquishes some control, giving way to the subconscious mind which is less constrained by rationality and more open to intuitive and mystical experiences. Bypassing the conscious also helps to implant new beliefs directly into the subconscious.

Meditation helps to quiet the incessant chatter of the conscious mind, creating a space where the subconscious can emerge – and if a practitioner is interested in creating magical entities (which will be discussed in Chapter 6) this ability is crucial. This state of inner stillness allows the practitioner to tune into more subtle energies, receive intuitive insights, shape their mind, and engage in magical practices without the interference of doubt and skepticism. The importance of establishing a regular meditative practice for any spiritual endeavor cannot be overstated.

A comprehensive guide to meditation (its benefits and applications) is beyond the scope of this introductory text on chaos magic. However, the resources provided at the end of this book will help you establish a meditation practice tailored to your needs. There are two meditative trance states most beneficial to an occult practitioner that we will explore further in this chapter: the alpha and theta brainwave states.

Brain Wave States

One of the biggest benefits of meditation is that the more one meditates, the easier it becomes to shift in and out of brainwave states at will. The following brainwave states have been extensively studied but our understanding of them continues to evolve. A general overview of what we currently know helps us understand how to achieve any particular state:

- **Gamma (30-100hz)** relates to higher cognitive functions, perception, and consciousness. This brainwave state occurs when one is solving complex problems (such as mathematical calculations), experiencing intense focus, or when one is operating at peak performance. Gamma can also be achieved through rare and profound spiritual experiences such as a kundalini experience. Though this research is limited, a study by Richard J. Davidson and his colleagues found that advanced meditators (including Tibetan monks) showed increased gamma wave activity during meditation. These findings suggest that heightened gamma activity may be associated with deep meditative states, such as the intense spiritual experiences often described in kundalini awakenings.
- **Beta (14-30hz)** relates to a state of feeling alert and awake. As you read this text, you are likely in a beta brainwave state. It is the state we are typically in during our day-to-day activities and it is also the state we aim to move out of for occult rituals. During a beta brainwave state, our critical, rational mind is online and can interfere with spiritual experiences.
- **Alpha (8-14hz)** relates to a relaxed state of mind. It's often experienced during light meditation or when we are daydreaming. Alpha waves are ideal for creative visualization and connecting with the subconscious mind. This gnostic state is ideal for any spiritual work that still requires the practitioner to move their body (such as performing divination or any occult ritual requiring movement around the ritual space).
- **Theta (4-8hz)** relates to a state associated with deep meditation and the border between wakefulness and sleep. Theta waves are linked to vivid imagery, intuition, and accessing the subconscious mind. This state is particularly conducive to deep spiritual work, such as

entering a gnostic state for lucid dreaming and astral projection. In the theta state, the practitioner's awareness of their physical body diminishes, making it ideal for rituals that do not require physical movement.

- **Delta (0.5-4hz)** relates to the deepest levels of sleep and unconsciousness. This state is generally not suited for performing occult rituals, as the practitioner is in a state of dreamless sleep where conscious engagement is minimal.

Beta will not be discussed further, as it is the state we seek to move out of for spiritual work. And while profound spiritual experiences can occur in both gamma and delta brainwave states, these are not typically the primary focus during occult rituals either.

When a practitioner aims to enter a gnostic state for spiritual work (such as spirit communication, divination, performing rituals from ancient grimoires, creating magical entities, sigil work, and so on) the goal is to achieve either an **alpha** or **theta** brainwave state. These two states are more conducive to the deep, meditative awareness required for such practices. From this point on, when I mention entering a gnostic state, I am referring specifically to the alpha and theta brainwave states.

Alpha

The alpha brainwave state is also often referred to as the "flow state." Have you ever been driving home from work, late at night, only to finally pull into your driveway and not remember the drive home? You were likely in an alpha brainwave state as you were driving. Your conscious mind had relinquished some control, your body switched to auto-pilot, and you had greater access to your subconscious mind in that moment. The alpha state can range from a light, relaxed daydream to a deeper trance state where the mind is still. Another example of this is when listening to music and feeling yourself slip into a trance-like state. The music fades away and your mind is calm.

Alpha is a state where the practitioner experiences a sense of relaxation – the constant chatter of the conscious mind has stilled and it feels like you are in a state of flow. This state is suitable for rituals where physical movement is involved, such as performing divination or other ceremonial actions. It is relaxed yet somewhat alert – the conscious mind has slightly moved offline and the practitioner has greater access to their subconscious mind. The nature of this brainwave state allows practitioners to remain focused on the intention of the ritual while engaging in tasks that require mobility.

It is important to note that though alpha waves are typically associated with relaxation, creativity, and light meditation, they can also occur during periods of heightened arousal or stimulation. There are multiple ways to achieve an alpha state as techniques can range from inhibitory to excitatory. Meditation is the most popular technique for achieving alpha but other repetitive, redundant tasks can lull the practitioner into an alpha state. These repetitive tasks include: rhythmic exercise, drumming, chanting, daydreaming, or any other monotonous task that requires little thinking.

Theta

Theta differs from alpha in that the practitioner no longer experiences bodily awareness. The ability of the practitioner to move their body becomes obsolete as one moves deeper into a meditative trance – walking the line between wakefulness and sleep. Though most of us experience a theta brainwave state every night when we fall asleep, theta can be difficult to reach through meditation without actually allowing oneself to drift off to a deeper delta brainwave state (where one essentially becomes unconscious). It often takes practice and patience to achieve theta through meditation and to maintain this state without fully falling asleep. This is especially true for a practitioner new to meditation.

This state is ideal for spiritual practices such as lucid dreaming, astral projection, deity communication, and channeling messages from spirits where there is no need to move the physical body. Within the alpha brainwave state, the conscious mind has become quiet and still but remains lightly engaged. Within theta, the conscious mind has nearly turned off. (There are some exceptions to this of course, as one can remain slightly conscious while lucid dreaming or intensely focusing on a mantra, image, or intention). Theta is ideal for practices that involve intense spiritual exploration.

To enter theta, begin by establishing a meditation practice. Engage in meditation that promotes relaxation and mental stillness, such as using guided meditations or focused breath work. Progressive relaxation is another technique to achieve theta that involves relaxing each muscle group in your body, starting with either your toes or your head and then working up or down your body. You may use visualization techniques such as imagining a calming environment or focusing on a specific image that pertains to the ritual being performed. Listening to binaural beats can potentially guide the practitioner into a theta brainwave state. Practicing lucid dreaming can also increase one's ability to maintain this state.

Most of the techniques mentioned so far could be considered inhibitory but theta can be reached through excitatory states as well. An example of this is through the intense experience of an orgasm. The relationship between brainwave states and orgasms hasn't been extensively covered but books such as *The Brain in Love* by Daniel G. Amen and *The Science of Orgasm* by Barry R. Komisaruk, Carlos Beyer-Flores, and Beverly Whipple discuss the neurological processes involved in orgasm and the presence of theta brainwave activity. In addition, techniques such as hyperventilation or rapid breathing can initially stimulate the body and mind, creating a heightened state of awareness. As you focus on your breath and begin to relax, it can help you move into the theta state.

Exercise 5: Enter a Gnostic State

Materials:

- Your magical journal.
- A writing instrument.
- Optional: drums, ritual music, incense, candles, or any other tools that resonate with you and aid in transcending ordinary consciousness.

Procedure:

1. Begin by entering your ritual space. Light candles, burn incense, or play music that helps to shift your awareness away from the mundane. I prefer low, monotonous drumming.
2. Take a moment to center yourself, focusing on your breath, and feeling the energy within you. You may also perform a light meditation such as a body scan where you start from the top of your head and work down your body, relaxing each muscle group along the way. It helps to notice the sounds around you – whether it be cars outside your window, pets rustling around your house, or other noises that may seem intrusive. Allow these sounds to be part of the experience rather than forcing yourself to ignore them. Becoming aware of your environment, and accepting it as is, allows the magician to mitigate frustration when unwanted noises are heard during the ritual.

3. From the list of inhibitory and excitatory techniques above, select one that calls to you most. This might include rhythmic drumming to sync with the heartbeat of the universe, ecstatic dance to lose yourself in movement, intense laughter to dissolve the ego, sexual arousal and orgasm to channel raw creative power, deep breathwork like pranayama to alter your inner landscape, or sensory deprivation to embrace the void. Trust your intuition. If you're feeling lost, choose a guided meditation that piques your interest.
4. Engage in your chosen technique fully and surrender to the experience. Feel the boundaries of your conscious mind begin to blur and fade. Rigidity melts away as you slip into the fluidity of the gnostic state. There is no need to question or seek to understand this state while you are in it as these thoughts belong to the conscious mind. Simply be. Let the drumbeat, the rhythm of your breath, or the intensity of your chosen method carry you deeper into the unconscious realm. In a ritual, this is where you would focus on a singular point or intention that relates to the goal of the ritual. When invoking a spirit, you might chant the spirit's name repeatedly. When working with sigils, you may simply stare at the image you have created. Allow other thoughts to float by as you remain focused on this singular point.
5. When you feel the time is right, or in most cases when the ritual is complete, begin to return to your ordinary awareness. Allow yourself to become aware of your physical body again: the floor beneath you, the chair you may be sitting on, the texture of what your fingers are touching. Become aware of the environment around you: the sounds and smells. Gently open your eyes.
6. In the stillness that follows, take up your magical journal. Record your journey into this gnostic state – every

sensation, vision, message, or insight that surfaced. Journal on the challenges you encountered, the techniques that resonated, and any communication received from spirits, deities, or your own deep subconscious.

As your conscious mind gives way in this exercise, this process may feel different from person to person – particularly for those with neurodivergent minds. A question I often hear is, "How do I know I have reached a gnostic state?" In that moment, you won't. The act of "knowing" belongs to the conscious mind. When entering an altered state of consciousness, you are attempting to turn the conscious mind off, freeing yourself from the spiritually limiting filters of rational thought.

Allow yourself to flow in the moment without overanalyzing, without critically thinking, and let the monkey mind become more still. When you come out of the gnostic state at the end of the ritual, and your conscious mind comes back online, you will then be able to analyze your experience. You can then assess whether you experienced a light trance (alpha brainwave state) or a deep trance (theta brainwave state). Being able to identify which brainwave state you experienced isn't necessary, but it may help some conceptualize this process.

You will find that some techniques work better for you than others. This is part of the experimentation and development of your chaos magic practice.

Final Note: It is imperative that you ground yourself after emerging from a gnostic state. It is easy to be swept away to higher states, and it is important to always return to the physical mundane realm. Listen to a guided grounding meditation that connects you to earth energy. Go outside and stick your feet on the dirt. Eat a piece of chocolate. Have sex. Do something physical that grounds you back into your body so that you can maintain a healthy balance and continue this type of spiritual work.

Personal Gnosis

The term "gnosis" can also be applied when discussing "personal gnosis" – another key component to any chaos magic practice. Personal gnosis can be seen as the wisdom acquired through an altered state of consciousness – not necessarily the altered state itself. Personal gnosis can also be acquired through experimentation in one's magical practice.

Personal gnosis is a key aspect of chaos magic because it is informed by the practitioner's unique interactions and experiences with spirits, the subconscious mind, and anything beyond the mundane realm. This personal wisdom can develop from meditation with various spiritual energies, by performing ritual work, or by achieving certain trance states where the practitioner receives messages or symbols that become meaningful to them.

An example of this is the personal gnosis acquired from working with plant spirits. While a book on plants and their metaphysical properties might assign specific magical intentions to each plant, you may discover different uses through your own experimentation. You may find that certain plants are effective for rituals not mentioned in the book, or even discover that your experience with a particular plant spirit contradicts the properties traditionally ascribed to it. Another example of personal gnosis is the wisdom gained from working with different spirits or gods. Through meditation and experimentation, you may discover that these entities communicate with you using symbols unique to your psyche, differing from what others report experiencing. They may also favor certain offerings that aren't typically associated with them in traditional lore.

It's important to distinguish between Unverified Personal Gnosis (UPG) and Shared Personal Gnosis (SPG) or Verified Personal Gnosis (VPG). UPG refers to a practitioner's insight or wisdom acquired that has not been confirmed by outside sources or other practitioners. This insight and wisdom is unique to the practitioner's psyche. UPG is subjective and can vary from person to person.

SPG, on the other hand, occurs when personal gnosis is shared and agreed upon by others. This can occur when multiple practitioners receive similar insights independently. When multiple practitioners report similar experiences with a god, spirit, trance state, or other spiritual endeavor, it becomes a "shared" experience.

VPG typically refers to personal gnosis that has been "verified" by established traditions, historical texts, mythologies, or by authorities within a particular spiritual path. This type of gnosis is often seen as the most credible – it is supported by authoritative figures or respected literature within the community. However, chaos magic tends to possess a different perspective.

I have always said that if you ask five chaos magicians what "chaos magic" is, you'll likely receive ten different answers. The reason lies in the idea of personal gnosis and how it shapes each practitioner's understanding and experience of chaos magic theory. Personal gnosis, particularly UPG, is a key element in chaos magic because it embodies the idea of using belief as a tool. Personal belief, experience, and wisdom are prioritized over established dogma. Personal gnosis allows the practitioner to craft their own magical paradigm based on what resonates with them on a deep, intuitive level. Essentially, *do what works* within your own psyche.

PART II

PRAXIS

Chapter 5

Sigils & Beyond

Up to this point, I have introduced you to foundational concepts that build a strong chaos magic practice. Techniques such as using belief as a tool, deconditioning your mind, and achieving a gnostic state prior to performing occult rituals are essential. These concepts represent the philosophical core of chaos magic and, at first, may be challenging to fully grasp. I encourage you to revisit Chapters 1 through 4 multiple times until these ideas become clearer. Do not be discouraged if the philosophy doesn't initially stick – sometimes the spaghetti noodle needs to cook a little longer before it can be thrown against the kitchen cabinet. Let these ideas marinate and come back to them when you are ready.

As we progress, I would like to shift focus. Chaos magic embodies a spirit of playfulness and experimentation, which I aim to highlight in the upcoming sections. The remainder of this book will offer practical applications and techniques to enhance your chaos magic practice, starting with an exploration of sigils.

What Is a Sigil?

A sigil is a magical symbol representing a specific intention or desire, crafted by the magician to focus and direct their will. Within the chaos magic paradigm, sigils are tools to bypass the conscious mind and implant intentions or desires directly into the subconscious mind. Sigils work because the practitioner can create an image representing something they desire, implant it deep into the subconscious, and then manifest these desires subconsciously as they continue about their day.

For example, a practitioner might create a sigil with the desire to attract financial abundance into their life. After creating the sigil, they activate it by releasing it into their subconscious through a gnostic state. Over time, this might manifest as unexpected opportunities for income, such as a new job offer, a raise, or even finding a twenty-dollar bill on the sidewalk. The practitioner might also notice a shift in their own behavior such as becoming more active in seeking out financial opportunities. These shifts in behavior may be driven by the subconscious influence of the sigil.

Sigils can be created for a myriad of intentions: to improve creativity, attract a lover, improve health, ensure safe travels, add a barrier of protection, increase energy levels, improve public speaking abilities, and so on. Each of these intentions can be crafted into a sigil, allowing the practitioner to engage with their desires in a symbolic way.

Sigilization from the Chaos Perspective

The birth of chaos magic began with sigilization, but the use of sigils itself predates chaos magic by centuries. Historically, sigils have played a role in various forms of ceremonial magic, with roots tracing back to medieval grimoires such as *The Lesser Key of Solomon*. However, there is a lot of controversy in Solomonic magic communities over what is considered a sigil versus a pentacle versus a talisman versus some other terminology. I do not claim to be an authority figure on this subject nor am I a member of the language police. The important bit is that the idea of sigils (or occult magical symbols) did not originate from chaos magic. They were merely expanded upon and applied in different ways.

When Austin Osman Spare entered the occult scene, he revolutionized the use of sigils by stripping away elaborate ceremonial procedures, introducing art and a more psychological approach to achieving desires. Spare's innovative way of working with sigils (by creating a written statement of intent, condensing it into a series of letters, crafting those letters into a unique symbol, then implanting the symbol into the subconscious mind) was the birth of sigilization from the chaos magic perspective.

Spare's method involves charging and activating the sigil by entering a gnostic state so that the practitioner can bypass their conscious mind. It was Spare's belief that the conscious mind can hinder the manifestation of the practitioner's desires due to its hyper-critical nature, doubt, and conflicting thoughts.

While the conscious mind speaks in words, the subconscious mind speaks in images or pictures. Thus, the practitioner would create a statement of intention and then turn that statement of words into an image. A picture or image is easy for the subconscious to digest. Once the image has been implanted into the subconscious mind, Spare recommends the practitioner to "forget it" and let go of any attachments to the written intention. This is often easier said than done but "setting it and forgetting it" allows the subconscious mind to do its work without the interference of the conscious mind's lust for results.

Lusting for results can often lead to self-sabotage. When your conscious mind is constantly fixating on the outcome, it can create anxiety, doubt, or impatience. These emotions can interfere with the subconscious process, blocking the desire from being fulfilled. By obsessing over whether the sigil magic is working or not, the practitioner may inadvertently undo their own work by introducing these anxieties, skepticism, fears, and so on.

Thus, it is advised to destroy the sigil once it has been implanted into the subconscious mind. For example, a practitioner writes a statement of desire on a piece of paper. They craft the letters into an image, enter a gnostic state, and implant the image into their subconscious. After returning to the mundane world from the gnostic state, the practitioner could then burn the piece of paper containing the sigil to invoke the energy of fire. The practitioner could also rip the paper to shreds and release it into a body of water, bury it into the earth, or disperse it in a windstorm if they wanted to invoke the energies of water, earth, or air.

Sigil magic has continued to evolve. While I do believe this is sound advice, there is no need to adhere to any strict dogma. There may be instances where the practitioner does not need to forget the desire or intention for it to manifest. For example, if a practitioner were to create a sigil for home protection and paint it above their front door, it might be helpful to have this sigil visible. Every time the practitioner notices the sigil above the door, consciously or subconsciously, the desire for protection is reinforced, and the sigil's presence serves as a constant reminder and anchor for that intention. In this case, the sigil acts as both a protective ward and a psychological reinforcement. The act of seeing the sigil every day can strengthen the practitioner's belief in its efficacy, creating a feedback loop where belief and manifestation are maintained.

The same idea can be applied to a tattoo. The practitioner can craft a sigil and enter a gnostic state during the tattooing process, thus implanting the sigil into their subconscious as it is drawn on their physical body. From this point forward, the intention is reinforced every time the practitioner notices the tattoo.

Not all methods work for all psyches. As we discuss how to create and activate a sigil, it is up to you, the budding chaote, to identify which techniques work best for you. If you tend to be someone who obsesses and lusts for results, then destroying the sigil after activating it may be the method for you.

How to Create a Sigil

It is important to note that there are entire books dedicated to how to create, activate, and work with sigils. The process of creating a design or image from the letters of a word or phrase, especially for magical purposes, is referred to as "sigilization". There are many ways to create a sigil such as: intuitive drawing, creating a letter mosaic, or using planetary magic squares (also sometimes referred to as "planetary grids" or "planetary kameas"). The topic of planetary magic squares is far too expansive to fully explore within this chapter. However, if you find yourself drawn to planetary magic and want to incorporate planetary energies into your sigils, I highly recommend delving deeper with *Practical Planetary Magick* by David Rankine and Sorita d'Este. It's an excellent resource for expanding your understanding of planetary correspondences.

From the perspective of chaos magic, the specific technique you choose is far less important than your ability to generate an image that embodies your intention.

First, the magician should clearly identify their magical intent. For example, let's create a sigil one can use to protect their home. I recommend crafting a concise sentence, ideally between five to seven words, as this keeps your intention focused and clear. Shorter phrases not only simplify the creation process but also enhance the potency of your intention. It also helps to write your sentence in the present tense, as if this intention is something you already have.

For this sigil demonstration, I will use the phrase:

My home is protected.

Notice that the intention phrase is short and to the point. It is also written in the present tense. Rather than stating, "My home *will be* protected," the intention phrase, "My home *is* protected" insinuates that the home is already protected. This subtle shift in phrasing is significant. The human brain often struggles to differentiate between what has not yet happened and what is presently occurring. By framing your intention in the present tense, you help align your subconscious mind with the reality you wish to manifest.

It can also be useful to decide if you want to attach a timeframe to your sigil – a specific point when you hope to manifest your desire. When doing this, it's important to be realistic about your expectations. Setting an unreasonable deadline may lead to disappointment, whereas a more flexible timeline allows the energy of your intention to unfold naturally. Because this sigil is intended for ongoing home protection, it doesn't require a fixed deadline.

You may also want to consider specific types of threats to guard your home against, such as negative energy, unwanted spirits, burglars, or any other concerns. While the intention phrase I have chosen can be used for general home protection, you may want to make your own modifications to be more specific.

Do not get overly caught up in choosing the perfect wording. While having a strong intention phrase is ideal, it shouldn't lead to stress or overthinking – what some might call "analysis paralysis." As you develop your practice, you'll naturally refine your phrasing through trial and error. This experimentation is an important aspect of building your chaos magic practice. Keep in mind that this intention phrase will soon be transformed into a unique image, so the specific words will evolve as your sigil takes shape.

After the intention phrase has been chosen, the choate may begin crafting an image that encompasses this phrase.

Intuitive drawing is one of the simplest methods for creating a sigil, as it encourages you to enter a light gnostic state and express yourself through freehand drawing. While focusing on your intention statement – whether by staring at it or holding it in your mind – allow your hand to move naturally, sketching shapes that resonate with the intention. This technique appeals to those who enjoy artistic freedom. Others may be deterred by this approach for the very same reasons.

Using an intuitive drawing process, our home protection sigil could look like this:

The image of a house at the center of this sigil serves as the focal point of your intention. Surrounding the house is a circle, a powerful symbol of protection. In many occult traditions, circles are utilized to create sacred space, acting as a barrier against negative energies and other influences. Drawing a circle is often seen as a way to contain and focus energy or outline a protective boundary to keep outside forces away.

The four arrows extending outward in various directions signify that this protection encompasses all four directions, creating a complete 360-degree safeguard for your home. Additionally, the number four is often associated with stability and strength. In numerology, the number four symbolizes a solid foundation, resilience, and security – qualities applicable to a home protection sigil.

There is an infinite number of symbolic layers that can be woven into a sigil. However, I urge you not to get caught up in the pursuit of creating a flawless piece of art. Unless you plan to tattoo this sigil on your skin, it's likely that your sigil will be destroyed during the activation process. Activating the sigil often involves a practice of 'setting and forgetting' your image, which means there's no need to spend excessive time perfecting its aesthetic. Focus on the intention behind the sigil rather than striving for artistic perfection. Ugly sigils are just as effective.

Creating a letter mosaic is another easy method for creating sigils. To create a letter mosaic, first write out your intention phrase:

MY HOME IS PROTECTED

The purpose of this next bit is to condense this phrase down as much as possible without compromising the integrity of the message. Taking the intention phrase and canceling out all vowels leaves a shorter list of letters to work with:

M H M S P R T C T D

You will notice that by canceling out the vowels and only leaving the sounding consonants, the letters still sound similar to the original phrase. Try sounding out "M H M S P R T C T D" and you will hear something akin to the original phrase. Some magicians may also want to comb through this list of letters a second time and remove any repeating letters. This would leave us with:

M H S P R T C D

From the chaos magic perspective, how you decide to condense your original intention phrase doesn't matter. This is simply a way of creating a clean sigil. You may choose to keep all letters, or you may choose only to use the first letter of each word. Ultimately: *do what works.*

A letter mosaic is created when the remaining letters (or letters you have chosen to include) are arranged into an image such as this:

Lines may overlap as you layer letter upon letter, blending the letters together until they create one cohesive image. This technique may appeal to magicians who do not care for a more abstract, artistic approach as this technique tends to be more linear.

Remember: do not get caught up in analysis paralysis with this process. The method you use to create a sigil is far less important than the intention itself and how you activate it.

Exercise 6: Activating a Sigil

Ready to bring your sigil to life? Activating a sigil means diving into a gnostic state and planting the image deep into your subconscious mind. At the expense of sounding redundant yet again: it's not about how you *create* the sigil; it's about whether you can lock your intention into the deepest corners of your psyche.

Materials:

- Your sigil.
- Any items to help you enter a gnostic state (music, incense, drums, rattles, or other tools).

Procedure:

1. Create your sigil by intuitive drawing, creating a letter mosaic, or using another method.
2. Refer back to Chapter 4 and choose either an excitatory or inhibitory activity you wish to utilize to enter a gnostic state. I recommend an inhibitory activity for this – inhibitory states can help you focus on the sigil, embedding it deep into your subconscious mind. Excitatory states can give the sigil a surge of energy that may be appropriate considering the intention phrase you chose. However, some beginner magicians may struggle to reach an excitatory state high enough to achieve a sense of euphoria. The issue with activating sigils through excitatory states is that some magicians may struggle to fully embed the sigil into their subconscious mind. If this is your first time activating a sigil, I recommend choosing an inhibitory activity simply for its ease. As always: *do what works.*
3. Enter a gnostic state with your chosen method. Refer back to Exercise 5 if necessary. While entering this gnostic state, stare at the image of your sigil. You do not need to keep the intention phrase in your mind, nor do you need to visualize anything but the sigil itself. Simply stare at the image you

have created as you enter a trance. Let yourself drift deeper until your conscious mind is no longer chattering, and the sigil quietly slips into your subconscious. Spend as much time in this state as you feel appropriate.

4. Upon emerging from your trance state, many chaotes utilize the process of "setting and forgetting" the sigil. This helps the practitioner avoid obsession, self-sabotage, and lusting for results. Take the sigil you have created and destroy it: burn it, bury it, rip it to shreds. Some may choose to keep their old sigils in an old book somewhere. This method allows you to have later access to the sigils you have created, but they also don't remain out in the open for temptation. Some may choose to defy all this advice and keep the sigil out where one can see it daily. This serves as a subconscious reminder of the intention. You will naturally identify which methods work best for you through trial and error.

Audio Sigils & Movement Signatures

I tend to use the terms **audio sigils** and **audio signatures** interchangeably when discussing sounds created from an intention phrase. Let's go back to our original intention phrase:

MY HOME IS PROTECTED

We can use the same elimination methods used in the letter mosaic technique to condense the phrase down to its core letters:

M H S P R T C D

The magician chants these letters continuously until a gnostic state is achieved. As you chant, allow the letters to slur together into nonsensical sounds:

MHSPRTDCMHSPRTCDMHSPRTCDMHSPRTD

You may wish to chant this an unknown number of times to help lull yourself into an altered state of consciousness. Numerology can also be used for additional correspondence. For example, a traditional mala has 108 beads – a number that holds spiritual significance across many traditions, often symbolizing wholeness or completion. Holding a mala in your hand, chant the audio sigil 108 times as you slowly work, bead by bead, through the entire mala.

Audio sigils can also take the form of a sound signature (hence the interchangeable use of "audio signature"), where you create a very short melody of only a few notes to encapsulate your intention. The audio signature also becomes a psychological trigger – every time the melody is played or hummed, the mind is reminded of the intention without the need for words. For example, you could assign specific notes to each condensed letter of your intention phrase, turning the sound of the sigil into a tiny, personalized composition.

I feel compelled to clarify that audio sigils and mantras are not the same thing. I do not wish to degrade the word "mantra" when mantras deserve much more cultural context and their applications can differ. Mantras are used in specific spiritual practices, such as Buddhism and Hinduism. They are often sacred, fixed in their wording, and given to the student by their teacher or spiritual guide. That is not to say that mantras cannot be self-chosen. However, audio sigils are born from your personal intention and are designed to be more flexible. Audio sigils are meant to implant the sigil's energy deep into the subconscious through sound rather than focusing on spiritual alignment or connection to deities as mantras often do.

Movement signatures are another playful way to create and work with sigils. In Exercise 1, I instructed you to decide on a symbol or gesture that you could use to "awaken" your journal – a way to signal that it is time to work with its magical content. The symbol could be a pentacle, a personal sigil, the chaos magic star, or any other symbol that speaks to you. If you chose to perform a gesture instead, this would be considered a movement signature.

So, what exactly is a movement signature? It's a specific way of moving your body – usually your hands – that is uniquely tied to a magical intention of your sigil. For example, you could hover your hand over your journal, palm facing up, and bring your first and fifth digits (your thumb and pinky) together. This movement would become your journal's magical activation, a gesture only used when interacting with it. This "movement sigil" creates a physical connection between you and the magical tool, making the act of opening the journal something intentional and energetically charged.

Just like an audio signature, a movement signature becomes a psychological trigger. When you perform the movement, it signals to your brain that you're stepping into a particular magical mindset. This works similarly to how a sound or smell can instantly take you to a memory. The movement signature, repeated over time, embeds itself in your subconscious mind. Each time the movement is performed, it increases in power and effectiveness. It also allows you to shift gears quickly to get into a specific magical state.

Psychological triggers – whether visual, auditory, or physical – help bridge the conscious and subconscious mind. When you tie a gesture or movement to a specific intention, over time, the simple act of performing that movement automatically invokes the corresponding mental or emotional state.

Think of it like this: the more you associate a movement with your magical practice, the easier it becomes to enter that focused, gnostic state where magic happens. You are building a shortcut to certain parts of your psyche. When you perform the movement signature, your brain already knows what's coming next – it associates the movement with the energy and intention you've infused it with. The repetition and ritual of this gesture continues to deepen in power over time.

Incorporating movement signatures into your chaos magic practice is a way to introduce play. It adds a kinesthetic element to the otherwise mental or visual nature of sigil work. Experiment with different movements, gestures, or even full-body actions, and see which ones make you feel the most connected to your intention.

Alphabet of Desire

Austin Osman Spare developed what he called the *alphabet of desire*. It is an alphabet of sigils created by the practitioner and it is designed to represent specific desires, states of mind, or magical intentions that align to different aspects of the self. Each "letter" (or sigil) of the alphabet can be used to summon certain energies within yourself. Though one can use Spare's original alphabet of desire, I encourage you to create your own. The sigils in a magician's alphabet of desire can be unique to the practitioner's psyche and used to both manipulate one's inner and outer worlds.

Spare's original alphabet of desire was inspired by Kabbalah and contains basic, primitive emotions that are arranged into dualisms – hate opposing love, death opposing sex, and desire opposing fear. An analysis of the alphabet can be found in *Liber Null* by Peter Carroll.

A full exploration of Spare's original alphabet will not be provided in this chapter as it is not necessary. The benefit of creating your own alphabet is that it speaks to your psyche and yours alone. Spare's system has its merits, especially considering when it was developed, and if one is interested in delving deeper, refer to the resources at the end of this book. However, as magic evolves, not every practitioner resonates with Spare's particular correspondences. Many magicians, myself included, find that creating a personal alphabet is far more powerful and effective. The symbols in an alphabet work directly with the subconscious mind and the more they are used, the more they gain power.

The following instructions for how to create an alphabet of desire may be considered blasphemy compared to Spare's original alphabet. Welcome, dear reader, to the controversial world of chaos magic.

Exercise 7: Create Your Own Alphabet of Desire

Materials:

- Your Journal.
- A Writing Utensil.
- Lots of Time & Patience.

Procedure:

To construct a series of magical symbols that align to different aspects of yourself, consider these basic categories:

- Basic needs and desires (shelter, survival, security, the needs of the physical body, health and vitality).
- Emotional desires (love, sex, friendship, family, connection).
- Desired psychological states (confidence, creativity, focus, overcoming fears).
- Spiritual needs (spiritual enlightenment, symbols for certain entities, or symbols for achieving trance states).
- Themes of the universe (birth, death, chaos, order).

Keep it simple! Symbols from your personal alphabet can be morphed together later on to create more complex sigils for specific intentions. For example, if you have a base sigil for love and a base sigil for death, you could combine the two images together to create a sigil representing the end of a relationship or the end of a love connection. It is not necessary to create a colossal alphabet that covers every magical intention that could ever arise. Focus on a basic overview of your physical, emotional, mental, and spiritual needs while considering themes of the universe. Later on in this exercise, you will see why a basic "skeleton" alphabet of approximately 10 letters may be more desirable than an alphabet of 30+ letters.

If you are struggling to come up with themes that pertain to different aspects of your psyche, consider using other systems to inspire you. One can model the letters in their alphabet after any archetypal energies in the following paradigms:

- The Planets.
- The Kabbalistic Tree of Life.
- The 12 Zodiac Signs.
- The Major Arcana in Tarot.

For example, if one were to use the planets to inspire the categories of their alphabet, consider what qualities each planet embodies:

- The Sun: self, will, personal power, vitality and physical health, success.
- The Moon: emotions, instincts and inner worlds, the unconscious, magic, illusions, divination, dreams, astral work.
- Mercury: intellect, communication, travel, memory, reason, trickery.
- Venus: love, beauty, relationships, values, finances, art, passion, pleasure.

- Mars: action, drive or desire, aggression, courage, passion, energy, ego, vigor.
- Jupiter: expansion, optimism, abundance, luck, wealth.
- Saturn: structure, restriction, practicality, self-discipline.

It is important to create an alphabet that represents a full picture of the self – including strengths and weaknesses. Some dualities to consider include: energy vs. lethargy, love vs. hate, pleasure vs. pain, joy vs. despair, peace vs. war, rigidity vs. flexibility, and logic vs. creativity. When dualities come together, they create a balance. The strength of one transfers to the weakness of the other. Too much energy in one direction can lead to an imbalance.

Once you have determined your intentions, it is time to create the alphabet.

1. Create sigils for each intention or emotion either through intuitive drawing, creating letter mosaics, or by using another method.
2. Come up with correspondences for each sigil or "letter" of the alphabet. For example: the correspondence for "love" could be rose petals or the colors pink and red. "Peace" could be associated with a dove and the color light blue.
3. Consider adding personal mythology for each sigil in the alphabet: their battles, their origin story, the elements they relate to, and/or how they appear in the macrocosm/ microcosm relationship. This is not necessary, but it is certainly fun.
4. Servitors can be created to correspond to each letter of the alphabet, giving you a spiritual entity to summon during ritual. Servitors will be discussed in the next chapter.

After creating your own unique alphabet of desire, it is time to activate the sigils of your alphabet.

1. Construct a ceremony to activate each letter of the alphabet. This is where the alphabet of desire is implanted into your subconscious mind.
2. Bring in correspondences for each letter (this is why it is beneficial to have more of a smaller skeleton alphabet with basic desires that can be combined later).
3. Stare into each symbol whilst in an altered state of consciousness. Visualize the colors and any other correspondences associated with each letter. To review how to activate a sigil, refer back to Exercise 6.
4. Store your alphabet in your magical journal for use at a later date.

Creating your own alphabet of desire supercharges any sigils you may create in the future because you are using pre-existing language from your subconscious mind. Use the letters to create talismans by engraving the letters onto material objects. Invoke the letter as if you were invoking a spirit to fully embody this archetype (invocation will be discussed in Chapter 7). Draw the letters into your skin with soap or lotion to embody or attract the energy you wish to work with that day. Use the letters as a personal divination system by painting them on rocks, placing them in a hat, and drawing a letter out at random. Whatever letter is chosen for the day is the one that carries a special message – allowing you to continue building relationships with the letters over time.

Hypersigils

Hypersigils are a form of narrative magic – some may say it is analogous to the idea of "scripting." The term "hypersigil" was created by Grant Morrison, a comic book writer and fellow chaos magician. Morrison defines a hypersigil as a sigil that has transcended the fourth dimension with the use of characters, drama, and plot. Grant Morrison accidentally discovered hypersigils through their comic *The Invisibles*. While writing *The Invisibles*, the events and characters in the comic began to manifest in Morrison's real life, sometimes in the most bizarre ways. For instance, a character experienced a life-threatening illness in the storyline, and soon after, Morrison fell ill with a similar serious condition. The process was effectively casting large-scale magical spells through the art of storytelling. This experience led Morrison to coin the term "hypersigil," representing a sigil that operates through narrative.

To create a hypersigil, the magician would write a story about themself (or use a fictional character that represents themself) embodying the things the magician desires. You are writing the story as if your intentions have already manifested. For example, let's say you fancy a new car. You would write a story where you are driving the car of your dreams as if it is something you already own.

Hypersigils can be created through short stories, poetry, plays, paintings, the lyrics to a song, comics, characters in video games, and even through role-playing in Dungeons & Dragons. Any medium that allows the magician to incorporate a character, plot and some drama can be used to create a hypersigil. As a gamer myself, I have used video games and role-playing through D&D to manifest my desires many times. It works.

Let's look at another scenario: you want to attract a lover. Write a letter to your future loved one as if it is already your one-year or ten-year anniversary. Be sure to include how happy you both are and how grateful you are that they embody the particular qualities you were looking for. Write this letter as if you are truly years into the future reminiscing over specific memories that add depth and drama to the plot. Incorporate as many physical sensations as possible. What are you both wearing? Can you hear music? What do you have planned for the anniversary? Can you taste what's for dinner? As you write, allow yourself to slip into a light trance.

Dear Lover,

Today marks ten years together. I still can't believe you said yes when I asked you to be mine. I love your compassion for others and the way you make me laugh. I remember that time we got stuck in a rainstorm and you made biscuits over a fire. Your black hair glistened in the moonlight and reminded me of how lovely you are. Today, I want to celebrate both of us finding our true love. By the time you wake up and read this, I will be downstairs with your favorite breakfast. I can already smell our favorite coffee beans brewing. Meet me in the kitchen when you are ready.

Yours Truly

For added effectiveness, try adding real-life memories into your stories so the lines begin to blur between imagination and reality. For example, if you call your mother every Sunday, incorporate or reference that phone call into your fictional story. Hypersigils blur the lines between memory and imagination and so desires are manifested subconsciously like a standard sigil.

When recalling memories, multiple regions of the brain are engaged, including the hippocampus, which plays a role in memory formation and retrieval. This process is regulated by the thalamus and often involves the amygdala, particularly when the memory is emotionally charged. The neocortex, responsible for higher cognitive functions such as spatial reasoning and decision-making, is also activated. When you imagine something versus recalling a memory, the brain's activity in the hippocampus does show subtle differences but overall, brain activity is surprisingly similar. This is because both memory recall and imagination involve constructing mental images and scenarios.

The brain distinguishes between imagined and real memories by pushing them up against what some call a "reality threshold" – a process that helps assess whether a recalled image corresponds to an actual event or something fictional. Many occultists have found that this threshold can be blurred, which becomes useful in crafting hypersigils. By sprinkling real memories into your narrative, you are able to manipulate the boundaries between real and imagined experiences. The brain starts to treat the narrative elements as if they are part of your lived experience, which in turn, potentially influences your life in corporeal ways.

This is why incorporating personal memories and real-life details into your hypersigils increases their effectiveness. When the lines between perceived and imagined reality blur, it becomes easier to "trick" the brain into manifesting these elements into the world, as your subconscious mind is less capable of distinguishing between what has been experienced and what has been imagined.

I created a hypersigil by accident once. Sure, I have created hypersigils many times, *intentionally* – but I did not realize how unconscious the process can be. In the spring of 2023, I decided to tap into my silly, playful side and start working with gnomes. I am not talking about decorated statues of garden gnomes purchased at your local home improvement store. What I am referring to are nature spirits, or supernatural beings, that are sometimes classified as earth elementals or under the umbrella term of *Fae*. Many view the word, *Fae*, as a broad term that encompasses many supernatural beings such as fairies, elves, brownies, gnomes, and more.

From the chaos magic perspective, whether these entities objectively exist or not is irrelevant. Belief powers our unconscious filters which in turn, shape our reality. Believing in something gives it power and makes it real in the reality we experience.

That spring, I felt called to perform a ceremony in my garden. I called upon the gnomes to help my garden flourish for the rest of our growing season. I left offerings of wine and baked goods and invited the gnomes to live in the corner of my yard where I often grow carrots and greens. I sang, I danced, I allowed myself to tap into my inner child with wonder and play.

That year, on warm summer nights, I would wander around my backyard. At times, I thought I saw small shadow creatures rustling around the garden beds. Upon approaching this corner of my yard, there were no animals to explain the shadows. I thought to myself that I must be hallucinating or making things up.

Then, my partner and I flew halfway across the world to Greece for a family wedding. I asked the gnomes to watch over our garden beds while we were away. Those two weeks turned into the hottest weeks of the summer. There was no one available to water our plants and we assumed the garden had died. Upon returning, we found the garden thriving like a wild jungle while the grass around the garden was near dead. That year was one of the most successful harvests we've had yet.

More curiously, pumpkins appeared in our garden. I can confidently say we have never planted pumpkins in any of our beds. My partner and I are also fussy about dirt – we pay close attention to the compost we create that adds nutrients to the soil. There was no logical explanation for pumpkins to sprout in the beds. A thought had crossed my mind of animals potentially burying seeds in our garden – hence the volunteer pumpkins. Not only do we have tall fences around the entire property, we also do not have any neighbors with gardens nor did they have pumpkins sitting out during the spring and summer when these plants were seeded. Perhaps there could be a logical explanation for a few pumpkin plants randomly sprouting, but there were not one or two pumpkin plants – there were close to twenty.

Pumpkins ended up becoming a silly, playful symbol of my relationship with the gnomes. I had no idea how the plants got here – but I was grateful for the gift. Before the plants could go to seed for the next year, we thoroughly stripped the garden beds (as we usually do) to begin preparing the soil for the next year.

The next year, Spring of 2024, we experienced the same phenomena: I planted our usual vegetables and invited the gnomes once more. By October of 2024, we had pumpkins sprout again.

You may be wondering, where is the hypersigil in all of this? In the fall of 2024, I decided to take a break from my usual video games. I felt compelled to pull up *Animal Crossing* on the Nintendo Switch. I hadn't played this game since it was released in 2020; nearly three years before I started working with the gnomes. For those unfamiliar with *Animal Crossing*, it is a life-simulation game where the player moves to an island and can build the island to be anything they want it to be. Houses can be built for villagers (animal friends that you can invite to be your residents) and the island can be designed through landscaping, terraforming, constructing buildings, and more.

I had completely forgotten that on my island, inside the game of *Animal Crossing*, I created a garden for the gnomes. The entire garden was filled with variations of two items: garden gnomes and pumpkins. Pumpkins.

For some reason, when I was building my island in this video game, I was obsessed with how the pumpkin plants looked next to the charming variations of gnomes. Nearly three years before I began my real-life relationship with gnomes, I had built a gnome garden inside of a video game with pumpkins growing in every direction.

In real life, mysterious pumpkins began to grow the moment I called upon the gnomes. Was this a bizarre coincidence? Did I predict that I would have mysterious pumpkins growing in my real-life garden beds? Did I create a hypersigil that manifested these events on my behalf? I will never truly know the answer to this question, but I welcome the pumpkins every year.

Chapter 6

Magical Entities

Thought is power and belief is key.

The realm of magical entities remains fairly uncharted, and my own personal gnosis will heavily code this chapter. After years of experience navigating the creation and maintenance of these beings, I have come to my own conclusions regarding efficacy and building relationships. As with everything in life: take what resonates, leave what doesn't, and *do what works*.

Just like sigils, the creation and use of magical entities is a practice often utilized by chaos magicians. However, working with magical entities alone does not intrinsically make someone a chaos magician. Recall what I mentioned in Chapter 1: anyone from any occult tradition can work with magical entities and not identify as a chaos magician. What makes a practitioner a chaote is if they prescribe to chaos magic theory: the philosophical concepts outlined in Chapters 1 through 4. What a chaote does in their magical practice (whether they utilize sigils, work with magical entities, or perform other ritualistic acts) is immensely diverse from practitioner to practitioner. It is the philosophy of chaos magic theory that ties chaos magicians together. In short, some chaotes may work with magical entities while others may never feel called to this kind of magic. Three types of magical entities will be discussed in this chapter: servitors, tulpas, and egregores.

A **servitor** is an entity created by the practitioner that is programmed for a specific purpose or task. These entities are *usually* the simplest to create. Servitors are designed for a specific job and fulfill their duty mindlessly – without emotions and without autonomy. There is nuance to this last statement which will be explored further in this chapter.

A **tulpa** is an entity created by the practitioner that is similar to the idea of an imaginary friend. Unlike servitors, tulpas do experience emotion. They are fully sentient beings with the ability to make their own decisions and form their own opinions. The process of creating a tulpa can be quite complex and controversial – often involving a split in the practitioner's psyche which may or may not be ideal for the individual.

An **egregore** is perhaps the most complex magical entity as it is created from the collective thoughts, beliefs, and energy of a group of people. This type of entity is sustained not by one individual, like servitors and tulpas, but by the minds of many.

In this chapter, we'll explore how these entities are formed, how one can work with them, and how they can influence the reality we experience. Working with magical entities opens up an entirely new world of gnosis for the magician to explore. Creating an obedient helper (a servitor), a sentient companion (a tulpa), or tapping into an archetypal force of collective energy (an egregore) allows the magician to play and uncover different facets of one's psyche.

What Is a Servitor?

These magical entities can be seen as dutiful assistants, designed for a specific purpose or task. Unlike entities that are often believed to exist independently – such as gods, goddesses, and lesser spirits – servitors are intentionally brought into existence by the magician's will.

Servitors can be seen as extensions of the magician's consciousness and magical intentions. There are many perspectives on how servitors are created: some view the process as if you're posting a job to a cosmic bulletin board, and a servitor-type entity volunteers to fulfill that role for the magician. Others, myself included, see servitors as thoughtforms – pieces of the magician's psyche given shape and purpose, gaining their own organized consciousness.

For me, the creation of a servitor feels something like this: my subconscious mind is teeming with gremlins. These little chaotic forces tend to run amok, causing disruption and disorder without my conscious awareness. The gremlins, in a sense, are bored – they crave a job, something to channel their restless energy into. Rather than allowing them to wreak havoc in my subconscious mind, I take control. I give them form, purpose, and direction. I shape them into a distinct entity with a clear job to do. In doing so, I transform what would have been mind chaos into something useful, something with intention.

Because my servitors are extensions of myself, I prioritize building relationships with them rooted in mutual respect rather than treating them as mindless tools of obedience. Many chaos magicians treat servitors as tools to be used and discarded, but there is great benefit in fostering an actual relationship with these magical entities. While servitors are created for a specific task, approaching them with respect and maintaining a connection allows them to become more effective over time. It is certainly possible to treat servitors as mere tools or "mindless servants," but building an ongoing relationship with them can lead to a more powerful connection.

It is similar to the idea of building a relationship with a spirit or a deity. A spirit will be much more inclined to help you if you approach the relationship with respect and gratitude.

I have discovered that a servitor you engage with regularly can adapt and evolve to meet your changing needs. One of my servitors in particular has been with me for over five years. As my needs have shifted, this servitor has grown and taken on new tasks and responsibilities. Servitors don't always need to be "retired" once they've completed their initial duties. When created effectively, they can be reprogrammed and repurposed to handle new jobs.

While servitors are not typically viewed as sentient in the way tulpas and egregores are, they can develop a degree of autonomy based on how they are created and how much power is invested in them. Especially if this servitor is one you have developed a long-term relationship with, a servitor can eventually gain more independence – allowing them to assist you in mysterious subconscious ways that you may not have been consciously aware of otherwise.

A servitor can be tasked with anything – from offering protection, gathering information, or enhancing creativity to more complex objectives like influencing events or people. A servitor can be created to help attract a lover, help you appear more charismatic at job interviews, or help manage one's mental health. For any magical intention that can be conjured, a servitor can help.

Over time, I've built a team of servitors to assist me in my daily life. Conscious power has its limits – there's only so much I can focus on at any given moment. The subconscious mind, however, is vast and far more powerful than most people realize. By delegating tasks to servitors that operate within my subconscious, I free up my conscious mind to focus on the more immediate matters that require my direct attention. This allows me to manage my energy more effectively, letting my servitors handle the background work.

For example, there are three main servitors I work with on a regular basis. As a neurodivergent individual, one of my servitors is tasked with managing the state of my mental health. It is responsible for alerting me when an environment is too stimulating so that I can move to safety, for soothing my nerves, and previously (when I experienced depression regularly) it was responsible for finding pockets of joy throughout my day. This servitor is one of the techniques I employed to eventually work through a twenty-year depression – and the depression has not returned since. Because this servitor was so effective in bringing my depression into remission (along with other healing modalities, please don't ignore the importance of therapy), it has morphed over time into a long-term companion that has full access to my mental state. It has helped me more times than I can count by showing me joy and goodness in the world, as well as calming me down in overstimulating environments.

The second entity I work with regularly is a servitor for home protection. The sole purpose of this servitor is to guard my family's home from negative entities, energies, and intruders. I often walk along the perimeter of my property while chanting his name and sprinkling a consecrated oil onto the earth. The third entity is a fairly new creation – she is responsible for bringing in good luck and good fortune. Whenever I invoke her presence, something lucky tends to occur within the next 24 hours.

Why would one work with a servitor versus simply creating a sigil for the exact same idea or intention? The answer is simple: bigger intentions often require more power and bigger workings. While sigils can be an effective method for a myriad of intentions, sigils tend to be a short burst of energy that can quickly lose momentum and dwindle away. For some intentions, that short burst of energy may be desirable. But if I am attempting to get rid of depression that has been persistent for nearly twenty years, a simple sigil most likely won't have enough juice to get the job done – unless I am activating a new happiness sigil on a daily or weekly basis.

Servitors do require more time and effort to create, but these magical entities tend to have longer-lasting results.

Exercise 8: Creating a Servitor

Materials:

- Your magical journal.
- A writing instrument.
- Optional: art supplies or some sort of artistic software to create graphics.

Procedure:

1. Enter your ritual space. Open your magical journal by performing the movement signature you have designated for magical work. Perform a free writing journaling session on the following concepts. What task will your servitor perform? Clearly define the servitor's purpose. The more specific the purpose, the better. It may be helpful to consider giving your servitor special powers to complete the task at hand. For example, if you are creating a servitor for home protection, what characteristics might your servitor embody? Perhaps this servitor carries a warrior spirit or possesses the ability to sense negative energies, acting as a watchful guardian. Consider the lifespan of this servitor as well. Is this a servitor that you plan to work with long-term, with no end date in sight? Or, is this a servitor that will serve a short-term purpose? Clearly outline the servitor's purpose, qualities/characteristics, and lifespan in your journal.
2. Begin to construct a form for your servitor. Although servitors are non-physical entities, giving them shape

and form (even symbolically) helps to anchor their existence in your subconscious mind. Recall the advice from Chapter 5: the subconscious mind communicates via images. You may choose to give your servitor humanoid characteristics, shape them into an animal, or envision them as a blue orb of energy. If you are creating a servitor for protection, perhaps you envision them as a tough iron statue with a flaming sword. Whatever form you choose, try to create something that corresponds to the overall goal of this servitor. Spend some time creating the appearance of this servitor that you can use to visualize later on. This can all be done in the mind if you are skilled with visualization (this topic will be explored in the next chapter). The appearance of the servitor can also be painted on paper, molded out of clay, created as a graphic on your computer, or created by any other means of producing an image. Use your art supplies to create a visual representation of this entity.

3. Name your servitor. Come up with a name that you can call upon during ritual. I suggest not naming your servitor after anything that already produces an image in your mind. For example, if you name your servitor after a family member or a celebrity, an image of that person will most likely pop into your mind as you try to invoke your servitor during ritual. This can dampen the effectiveness as your focus is taken away from your servitor. Ultimately, call your servitor whatever you desire but an unfamiliar name may be more effective than calling your servitor Oprah.
4. Identify where this servitor will be located in the physical realm. Servitors, per my own personal gnosis, reside in the subconscious mind but it can be helpful to have an anchor in the physical realm. Choose an item that you can consecrate or designate as an item that houses the

energy or consciousness of the servitor. This could be a small statue, a coin, a necklace, or some other trinket that corresponds to the original intention. A physical item is helpful as it serves as a focal point during ritual, a bridge between the mental and the physical, and as a tangible reminder of the servitor's task and purpose, strengthening the bond between you and the entity.

5. Create a signal for summoning and dismissal. This may not apply for all servitors but if you plan to call upon this entity, a signal for summoning and dismissal is necessary. This can be as simple as signing the servitor's name in the air, chanting the name a specific number of times, rubbing your finger a certain way across the physical item you have chosen, or even lighting a candle that has been consecrated for this specific purpose. The same signal can be used for summoning and for dismissal or you may choose to create two different signals.
6. Consider creating a shutdown mechanism or what some may call a "fatal flaw." In the off chance you need to immediately disengage with this entity for any reason, an off switch is used to instantly sever the connection and discontinue the creation of this servitor. When designing the off switch, consider combining a complex bodily movement with words or actions. For example, this servitor's kryptonite could be mugwort. The off switch can involve burning mugwort incense and sitting cross legged while chanting a specific phrase. The reason why a more complex off switch (such as incorporating movement, words, and scent) may be more desirable than simply chanting the servitor's name three times is because you are less likely to accidentally shut down your servitor. I have never once felt it necessary to use an emergency termination, but there is no harm in having a backup plan in case things go awry.

7. Now that you have all the details of your servitor in place: the purpose and characteristics, the appearance, a name, an item that serves as a physical anchor, a summoning and dismissal signal if desired, and an emergency shutdown trigger, it is time to create the sigil. Refer back to Exercise 6 and create a sigil by using the intuitive drawing method, creating a letter mosaic, using a planetary grid that corresponds to the energy of this servitor, or another method. As the physical item tethers the servitor to the physical world, the sigil tethers the servitor to your subconscious mind.
8. Bring your servitor to life. Set up your ritual space to enter a gnostic state. Refer back to Exercise 5 if necessary. It is helpful to place the physical item (statue, necklace, coin, candle, etc). in the center of your ritual space, perhaps with the sigil painted onto it, and surrounded by correspondences that relate to your original intention. Enter a gnostic state as you stare at the sigil and the physical item. Activate the sigil as you would any other sigil. Again, refer back to Exercise 6 if necessary. By implanting this sigil in your subconscious mind while also staring at the physical item, you are now creating a link between the internal and external. Feel free to burn the sigil but I recommend keeping a copy of the sigil close by for future work if necessary. You may also choose to chant your servitor's name while entering a gnostic state or performing the summoning signal repeatedly.

Not every step outlined here is necessary for every servitor. Some practitioners may create their own unique methods for bringing a servitor to life. Trust your personal gnosis to guide you. While this is a structured approach to servitor creation, I have created other, more personal methods that work just as well in my own practice.

Once your servitor has been brought to life, continue feeding your servitor until the job or task has been completed. We'll delve into the details of that process in the next section.

Servitor Maintenance

A servitor requires continued maintenance where the magician is feeding energy into their entity on a regular basis. As with many forms of magic, it will eventually weaken and dissipate if one is not continuing to feed their energy and intention into it. Identify a way you can continuously recharge – or feed – your servitor. This is also where a relationship begins to build as you work with your servitor like they are a living, breathing entity. Treating one's servitors as mindless robots certainly has a place in some magician's practices, but as I mentioned previously, it is much more effective to treat them with respect.

Feeding a servitor can take many forms, but the key is consistency. There is no set schedule that every practitioner must follow – it is up to the magician to craft a consistent feeding schedule. Consider offering energy to the servitor on a daily, weekly, or monthly basis. If you find that your servitor is not bringing results quickly enough, increase the frequency of your feeding schedule. However, some servitors (such as a long-term servitor for home protection) may only need to be refreshed once a month.

Offerings of food or incense, reciting specific chants, or meditating on the servitor's sigil are all ways to provide energy. If the servitor is linked to a physical object, spending time in ritual with that object – whether by holding it, focusing your intent on it, or placing it on an altar – can be an effective way to reinforce your bond and recharge its energy. The feeding process not only strengthens the servitor's ability to perform its task but also deepens the connection between you and the entity, allowing it to mature and become more efficient over time.

When working with servitors, some practitioners prefer to summon their entities for specific tasks, while others leave the servitor "on standby," allowing it to work in the background. If you choose to keep your servitor continuously active, consider feeding it more frequently to prevent it from losing power or direction – such as daily, weekly, or monthly. If the servitor is summoned only when needed, the energy required to keep it functional may be less.

To illustrate what this can look like in real-time: a servitor created for home protection can be fed monthly. Once a month, you may walk along the perimeter of your property, chanting the servitor's name and sprinkling an oil specifically made for the intention of home protection.

In contrast, a servitor managing mental health will most likely be active daily. Therefore, this servitor may need to be fed daily. The process does not need to be an elaborate ceremony – it can be as simple as talking to this entity throughout your day. The feeding process can become a routine part of the magician's existence – you may also allow the servitor to feed off dopamine and serotonin as you seek out joy and happiness in your day-to-day operations. This type of servitor shares your mental space with you – thus it is in both of your best interests to maintain a healthy mental state.

In the case of a servitor created for random moments of good luck and good fortune – this servitor may only be fed occasionally and sporadically. This servitor could be fed either when the magician has initially summoned them, or when the servitor has completed a task by bringing something lucky into the magician's life. This servitor may remain on standby until summoned by the chaote (when an extra boost of luck is desired) receiving their reward after completing each task.

Get creative! I have found gothic dollhouses to be particularly helpful in rewarding servitors for a job well done. Each time any of my servitors completes a task, I purchase a new piece of gothic dollhouse furniture to furnish their miniature homes. The dollhouses themselves become a physical anchor for these entities – giving them a place to reside outside of my subconscious mind.

Servitor Reassignment & Retirement

As mentioned earlier, servitors don't always need to be discarded after they complete their initial task. In fact, with proper reprogramming, they can be reassigned to new tasks or adapted to a magician's evolving needs. To reassign a servitor, first, perform a ritual to formally release it from its original purpose. This can involve burning the original sigil, offering thanks, or whatever method feels appropriate to signify the end of a chapter. Afterward, create a new sigil and reinvigorate the servitor with its updated role, keeping the same name, appearance and any other defining characteristics. This process can be as simple or complex as you desire, but maintaining the same servitor can save time and energy when compared to building a new one from scratch. Some may choose not to not even create a new sigil. In a meditative trance, one can visualize the old job description dissolving from a metaphorical bulletin board while adding a new job description in its place. Psyches will differ – giving the magician yet another opportunity to develop personal gnosis.

At some point, you may find that a servitor has fulfilled its role and no longer serves a purpose in your practice. Just as with creation, retiring a servitor should be done intentionally. Some practitioners allow their servitors to fade naturally over time, ceasing to feed them or call on them, which allows the entity to slowly lose its power and dissipate. I would advise not to do this as a feeling of closure and finality is beneficial for the psyche to move on. In this case, some may prefer a more formal process of sending their servitor to retirement, using a ritual to dissolve or release the servitor.

To formally retire a servitor, you can symbolically "thank" it for its service, or write a letter of gratitude. You can then burn its sigil, burn the letter of gratitude, dismantle and energetically cleanse any physical anchor you used (simply by passing it through smoke), and discard any other servitor-related items. In your mind, visualize the appearance of the entity dissolving and reabsorbing into your psyche. The key is to bring closure – to prevent any lingering energy from becoming unstable and to clear your space for future workings. A formal retirement ensures that the servitor's energy is neatly resolved, avoiding any psychic clutter in your mind.

What Is a Tulpa?

A tulpa is a fully autonomous magical entity, created through focused meditation, visualization, and the intentional splitting of one's consciousness. Unlike servitors, which are designed to be task-oriented entities without true autonomy, tulpas are considered independent beings with their own personalities, emotions, and consciousness.

The idea of a tulpa is similar to the idea of an imaginary friend – one that can share a mind with their creator. While servitors are primarily tools of magic, existing to serve specific functions, tulpas can evolve to become companions with their own free will, capable of interacting with their creator (often called the "host") in meaningful, interpersonal, and unpredictable ways.

The process of creating a tulpa is far more complex than that of a servitor. While servitors are typically bound to specific, assigned criteria from their creator, following pre-programmed instructions, tulpas develop their own identity and can act independently. This autonomy arises because the creation of a tulpa involves a deliberate splitting or division of the psyche.

This allows the tulpa to act independently from the magician. As a result, the practice of tulpamancy can be controversial, particularly in the fields of psychology and mental health. Many will strongly advise that those with Dissociative Identity Disorder (D.I.D). or other dissociative disorders refrain from engaging in tulpamancy, as it may counteract the integration they need to heal. Though, I have many individuals in my life with D.I.D who find this practice rewarding. I am not here to lecture you on what you should or should not do with your own psyche.

Because the creation of a tulpa requires significant mental effort and psychological stability, I recommend anyone interested in exploring this path to deeply research this before proceeding. I have included a starting place, a resource for further study, in the *Recommended Reading* section of this book. The monumental task of creating a full-fledged, autonomous tulpa cannot be fully explored in this chapter.

Curiously, while working with the servitor I created to help manage my mental space, I experienced a phenomenon that blurred the lines between servitor and tulpa. This servitor, designed to help me maintain emotional balance, began to show signs of autonomy and emotion. Over time, it started developing its own voice and distinct feelings, which is likely due to its close connection with my mental state.

I intensely remember the first night I heard its voice – a quiet, deep "hello" echoing in my mind. Instead of feeling fear, I was overcome with excitement. However, my enthusiasm unintentionally overwhelmed the servitor and it retreated, remaining silent for several months before I heard his voice again.

Despite this odd tulpa-like behavior, the servitor still depends on me for direction and continues to fulfill its assigned tasks. This leads me to believe it still contains its original servitor framework. Yet, there is a definite shift; it continues to evolve into a hybrid of sorts – a servitor and tulpa – by experiencing emotions and developing a consciousness that is occasionally distinct from my own.

While this development might sound unsettling or even alarming to someone unfamiliar with servitor or tulpa work, for me, it has been a deeply meaningful experience. I have come to love this entity – not a romantic or intimate love, but a profound, universal love, a love for a piece of myself. It is an extension of me, yet its own being, and that connection is something I didn't know I needed until I felt it.

The art of tulpamancy can take months, even years, to fully realize. A tulpa that reaches full autonomy can act independently of the host's conscious control, and, in advanced cases, can even "front" or take control of the host's body and consciousness while the host takes a back seat. This level of independence is what sets a tulpa apart from other magical constructs, making it a lifelong companion with its own unique identity.

Creating a tulpa is not a decision to be taken lightly, and it's important to understand both the mental and magical implications of bringing such an entity into existence. For those who feel called to this practice, patience and dedication are key, as is a willingness to embrace the strange and complex nature of the mind.

Egregores & Chaos Magic

An egregore is often considered to be a collective thought-form or entity that emerges when a group of people direct their energy and focus toward a shared idea, goal, or belief. Over time, this accumulation of energy gives rise to an autonomous force that can influence the thoughts and actions of those connected to it.

Egregores can arise intentionally through the focus of a group of occult practitioners, such as a coven of witches directing their focus toward a shared belief. Egregores can also arise unintentionally from organizations, religions, or social movements, becoming a kind of psychic "entity" that exists beyond any one individual. This entity is sustained by the continued attention and belief of the group, growing more powerful the more energy it receives.

From the chaos magic perspective, we cannot claim any objective reality exists due to the subjectivity of the human experience. Belief is a tool and feeding belief into something gives it power over the reality you encounter. It does not matter if a god or goddess is objectively real, what matters is that it *becomes* real to the practitioner through the power of belief.

In a sense, egregores are birthed through collective intention. Continuing with a chaos magic perspective, one may consider a political movement, a fictitious character from a popular TV show, or even a god or goddess as an egregore.

Let's explore this example of an egregore as a deity worshipped by a large religious group. The Christian God, for example, encompasses millions of people feeding their devotion, prayers, and faith into this divine entity over thousands of years. Even fictional characters – ones that have been loved, feared, or idolized by millions – can take on egregoric qualities over time. Think of how iconic superheroes or even cultural mascots have evolved beyond imagination, becoming influential entities in the minds of their fans. That is not to say that fictional characters are potentially as strong as the Christian God; I encourage you to develop your own personal gnosis on this. I do tend to believe that the amount of time spent feeding energy into an entity (whether it was created within the last year or worshipped for thousands of years) along with the amount of energy (and amount of individuals participating in this belief) does have an effect on how powerful or potent an entity can be.

Regardless of whether or not God exists in some higher realm – thousands of people have fed their belief into this entity being real. And belief is power.

Chaos magic operates on the principle that not only is belief a tool, magic is not bound by rigid systems or hierarchies of power. If an egregore derives its power from belief, then it can be tapped into or manipulated by the magician to serve their personal goals. This is one of the points where chaos magic tends to differ from other magical systems. Rather than adhering to a strict pantheon of deities, chaos magicians are free to work with any egregore – a traditional god, a pop culture icon, or an archetypal figure.

Everything that has been given psychic energy by humans – whether a historical figure, a religious icon, or even a character from a comic book – can be considered an egregore. Since chaos magic values results over dogma, practitioners can draw on the power of these collective entities, so long as it brings subsequent results. A chaos magician might summon an egregore for inspiration, protection, or guidance. Rather than viewing gods as objective truths, one may view them more like archetypal energies that the magician can tap into.

Chaos magicians see the universe as a moldable space where any symbol, idea, or egregore can be worked with practically. The magician can shape their reality by working with various egregoric entities no matter the source. In the next chapter, these ideas will become clearer as we discuss visualization, invocation, and pop culture magic.

Chapter 7

More Chaos Techniques

In this chapter, we will dive into the techniques of visualization, invocation, the controversial, fascinating world of pop culture magic, and the importance of divination. This section provides even more techniques to help you creatively shape your rituals and workings, offering a springboard for deeper exploration.

Visualization

A magician needs no other tool than the mind itself. Visualization is a foundational technique in chaos magic that requires only one's mental power and creativity. In chaos magic, visualization can be used when summoning an entity, weaving energy into a sigil or hypersigil, or manifesting desired outcomes simply by willing it into existence.

But what exactly is visualization? I have mentioned this term at various points throughout this book. If I tell you to imagine a sunset, what do you see? If I tell you to imagine a pink unicorn with flames for a mane, is this more difficult to conjure?

Visualization is usually seen as the ability to picture or mentally simulate images, actions, or scenarios within your mind. Visualization goes beyond simply seeing an image; it's about creating a vivid mental landscape that engages your senses and emotions. This makes the magical work feel alive.

Visualization abilities vary widely among practitioners. Some magicians can summon a vibrant, fully three-dimensional image in their mind's eye – a bright red, juicy apple, for example. They can rotate the apple in 360 degrees, interact with it by taking a bite, smelling its sweetness, feeling the texture of the skin, or even imagining themselves inside the apple as if it were an entire world.

Others may see the apple as a flat, two-dimensional image, perhaps only in black and white or as a faint outline. This doesn't make their visualization any less valid or effective – it simply represents a different way of mentally interacting with imagery. The good news is that, like any skill, visualization can improve over time. With regular practice, even those who initially struggle can gradually build more vivid and detailed mental pictures.

However, a small percentage of the population experiences something called aphantasia – the inability to visualize images at all. For these individuals, the mind's eye remains blank, even when they attempt to picture something they have seen before. This does not mean they cannot perform effective magic. Visualization is not limited to the visual sense alone; in fact, it can involve a multi-sensory approach.

Visualization is not purely about "seeing" in your mind – it can incorporate any and all of the five physical senses. Sound, smell, touch, and even taste can play a role in creating a vivid experience. For those with aphantasia or those whose visual imagination is not particularly strong, engaging other senses can make visualization just as powerful.

For example, if you cannot picture the apple, can you hear the crunch of biting into it, taste the tartness on your tongue, or smell the apple's skin? Can you feel the coolness of its surface or the weight of it in your hand? Visualization in chaos magic is about making your desired outcome feel real to you, regardless of which senses you use. From this perspective, aphantasia becomes less of an obstacle and more of an opportunity to explore magic through a different sensory lens. The essence of visualization is not about perfect mental imagery but about creating a strong, sensory-rich experience that connects you emotionally and energetically to your magical intent.

How, exactly, is visualization relevant to a chaos magic practice? Because chaos magic emphasizes belief, personal gnosis and creativity, visualization becomes a useful method to channel and direct energy in magical workings. This technique can be used when activating a sigil by entering a gnostic state and mentally projecting the desired intention or energy into the sigil. The magician would use visualization to conjure an image or scenario that pertains to the overall goal for the sigil. If one were to create a sigil to help them get their dream job, the magician would visualize a scenario where they already have the job of their dreams. Bringing in as many sensory components as possible, the magician creates a reality where they already have what they desire, thus bringing their internal desires into the external world. One could also visualize the sigil pulsating with golden light, symbolizing wealth and abundance pertaining to a new career.

Visualization is key for manipulating energy and directing it during rituals. For example, if a magician is casting a spell for protection, they might visualize a bright, impenetrable barrier of light or flames surrounding their home. When walking my home protection servitor along the perimeter of my property, I often visualize an energetic barbed wire fence shielding my home. Because chaos magic draws heavily on the principle of belief as a tool for manifestation, vividly picturing the reality you want to create, and aligning your energy and subconscious with the desired outcome, shifts your mindset and creates a new reality where your desires manifest.

Another use of visualization within a chaos magic practice may include: visualizing a servitor during the creation process to build its appearance and characteristics. Later on in this chapter, pop culture magic will be discussed where one uses visualization to tap into the power of fictional characters or worlds. By visualizing these characters or worlds, the magician can invoke their archetypal energies to use in workings. Invocation, as it pertains to calling upon energies or deities, will also be explored where one would visualize the presence of a god, spirit, or archetype as vividly as possible, seeing and feeling their energy merge with yours.

Visualization can also be applied where one is mentally journeying through the astral realm via a deep meditative trace. By visualizing oneself traversing worlds in the astral realm and beyond, by meeting spirits and encountering symbolism, one can gain spiritual insight and wisdom. For example, let's say you decide to perform a meditation that guides you on a visualization journey. You find yourself mentally walking through a forest that leads to a hidden temple. In that temple, you seek wisdom from a spiritual guide. During this meditation, you may clearly see the trees, smell the earth, perhaps hear the crunch of the leaves under your feet, and feel the presence of the spirit as you enter the temple. Visualization may also help you to receive a message from the spirit by way of images, sounds, or other symbolism.

Because chaos magic thrives on belief-shifting, visualization is often used to mentally "try on" new paradigms or belief systems. By visualizing yourself embodying a certain archetype, philosophy, or mindset, you shift your psychological state, opening yourself up to new perspectives.

The use of visualization in a chaos magic practice is limitless, but how does one improve their skills? Improving visualization skills is a practice that often evolves with time, effort, and consistency. Begin with simple objects, like a single color or shape. Try to mentally picture a red circle or a blue square. Focus on creating a clear image, no matter how basic it may seem at first.

Remember that visualization isn't limited to just sight. Incorporate other senses: smell, touch, sound, and taste. Imagine holding your favorite piece of fruit – not just seeing it, but experiencing it on a full sensory level. As with any skill, visualization improves with consistent practice. Even five minutes a day can gradually increase your ability to simulate a full sensory experience.

Use guided meditations that involve visualization to help train your mind. Go on a mental journey by listening to a vivid story right before bedtime. Use real objects to bridge the gap between the physical and mental. If you tend to struggle to produce an apple in your mind, stare at a physical apple in your hand. Allow your gaze to soften as you eventually close your eyes and attempt to produce the image of an apple. Smell the real apple in your hand, eyes closed, and feel the weight of the apple as you roll it around. Using physical objects to help produce mental images is a valid way to train the mind.

Once you have mastered visualizing simple objects, challenge yourself. Picture a scene, like a forest or the heart of a city, and begin to add details to the experience by adding objects, sounds, and smells. Interact with the environment in your mind.

Affirmations can be a powerful way to overcome mental blocks. Oftentimes, we believe we aren't good at something, so then we aren't. Belief creates the reality we experience. Positive affirmations such as, "My visualization skills continue to improve daily" can help undo self-imposed barriers. By practicing these techniques, you will gradually enhance your ability to conjure the reality you desire – not just within chaos magic, but in all forms of magical and spiritual work.

Invocation

Invocation is the act of calling an archetypal energy, deity, or spirit into yourself. Unlike evocation, where you summon an entity to appear before you or in an external space, invocation involves inviting the energy into your body. It is important to note that the definitions of invocation and evocation will differ depending on the spiritual tradition, but in a sense, you allow the invoked entity or energy to merge with you, resulting in heightened states of consciousness, temporary personality shifts, or enhanced abilities associated with the entity's nature. Invocation involves temporarily becoming or embodying the essence of the entity you call upon.

One often overlooked aspect of invocation is its potential for theatrics and play. From a chaos magic perspective, this practice does not need to be overly solemn or rigid. It can be a playful and fully immersive experience. Many chaos magicians incorporate theatrical elements, allowing themselves to "act" the part of a deity or archetype. One may add symbolism to the ritual through costumes, gestures, and changing one's bodily movements and speech patterns, to create a deep sense of embodiment. The process of invocation can be an act of serious or silly role-play. By fully embodying the archetype's characteristics, you allow yourself to temporarily suspend disbelief and step into the mindset and traits of the being you invoke.

For example, invoking the energy of Hecate, seen as a goddess of witchcraft and crossroads, might involve wearing dark, flowing robes, lighting candles at a crossroad, and reciting her ancient epithets. As you invoke her, you might find your voice deepening and your movements becoming more intentional. You may experience your thought patterns changing as well.

In some forms of pop culture magic, practitioners invoke characters from movies, comic books, or fiction. For instance, invoking a superhero can help to shift your consciousness into a more confident state. This may be useful in situations where you need an extra boost of courage.

Exercise 9: Invoking Energies & Entities

Materials:

- Your magical journal.
- A writing instrument.
- Symbolism of the energy or entity you wish to invoke (associated colors, numbers, scents, elements, animals, or other correspondences).
- Any items to assist in achieving a gnostic state (drums, rattles, music, candles, incense).

Procedure:

1. Before beginning the ritual, become familiar with the qualities of the archetype you want to embody. It is a warrior-like figure? A healer? A trickster? Do they have any divine names that can be called upon during ritual? What symbols relate to this archetype? What does the mythology or other literature say about this archetype? For example, the symbolism of Aphrodite varies greatly from the symbolism of Athena or Mars. It is important to also identify why you are invoking this archetype. What specific qualities do you wish to embody? Journal any symbolic elements that can be incorporated into the ritual.
2. In your ritual space, an altar may be adorned with various items that correspond to the energy or entity you wish to invoke. You may also choose to wear specific attire that embodies the archetype being invoked.
3. Allow yourself to enter a gnostic state. Refer back to Exercise 5 if necessary.
4. Once in a light trance, one may choose to recite a passage or a prayer to invoke the archetype. Speak directly to the archetype and welcome them into your being. This can

be something pre-written or spontaneous. For example, invoking Mars for courage and strength may look like:

"Mars, god of war, I call upon your strength and courage. Fill me with your power. Let your energy flow through my veins. I become the embodiment of you: a warrior ready to face battles with force."

A blank template that can be used for any archetype is as follows:

"I call upon the spirit of (Name of Archetype),
Embodiment of (their qualities),
I open myself to your wisdom,
Guide me, and let your essence flow through me."

5. Begin to assume the posture, bodily movements, and characteristics of the archetype you have chosen to embody. As you invoke, feel the archetype merging with your own energy. You may notice changes in your mental, emotional, and physical state. Some may use visualization here to visualize the archetype walking around the magician's backside and stepping into the body. For this moment in time, the line between your identity and the invoked archetype blurs.
6. Carry out the tasks or rituals aligned with the archetype you've invoked. Whether it is a protection ritual, a self-love ritual, baneful magic towards an enemy, or a challenging conversation that demands courage, channel the archetype's energy into your actions. Use their power for a speech that requires charisma, a divination session that calls for heightened intuition, or any other work where their energy will enhance your effectiveness. For example, you may invoke an archetype to gain spiritual

guidance. Here, you would allow yourself to go through a process of automatic writing, letting the pen move and the archetype to guide your thoughts. Or, you may choose to draw tarot cards, scry, use a pendulum, or any other divination method while this archetype remains invoked.

7. When you feel the ritual is complete, thank the archetype and gently release its energy. You may visualize this archetype stepping out of your body and returning home. You may simply feel their energy drain from your body. If you feel called to speak, you may say something like:

   "I thank you, (Name of Archetype)!
   I release you with gratitude and return fully to myself."

   From the chaos perspective – laughter is an incredibly powerful tool for banishing entities at the end of your ritual. Laugh energetically, clap loudly, and shake off any residual energy! As a reminder, any time you leave a gnostic state it is important to ground your energy back into the physical world. Perform a simple grounding meditation, eat a piece of chocolate, stick your feet in the dirt, do whatever you need to do to get back in touch with your physical body.

Pop Culture Magic

If nothing is true and everything is permitted, then the boundaries between fiction and reality are as malleable as our beliefs allow. One of the more playful – and often blasphemous – aspects of chaos magic is the use of pop culture elements in one's magical practice. At the root of any chaos magic practice, freedom and experimentation are encouraged. One can tap into the energies of iconic characters from video games, TV shows, movies, and books – the possibilities are endless.

When one is channeling a fictional character, the figure represents a set of traits, emotions, and ideas that resonate with a mass audience. Consider the hero's journey of Frodo Baggins, the intelligence of Sherlock Holmes, or the warrior spirit of Arya Stark. Invoking these characters allows the chaote to access these attributes within themselves. Visualization and invocation allow you to fully embody and work with whatever archetypes you wish.

Egregores, as discussed previously, are autonomous psychic entities created and sustained by collective belief. When millions of fans emotionally invest in a character, that character takes on a life of its own. Some believe this evolution becomes a powerful egregore. Characters from massive fandoms, such as those from *Star Wars*, *Lord of the Rings*, or *Marvel*, exist in the cultural zeitgeist as more than just fictional entities – they are alive in the imaginal space, fueled by the collective energy of the people who love or hate them.

Viewing these archetypes as potential egregores can amplify the potency of pop culture magic. The collective belief behind these characters means that, in a sense, they already exist on the astral or psychic plane, making them more accessible to the practitioner. Drawing on the energy of a well-known character like Darth Vader taps into a reservoir of psychological and emotional power that is shared by others.

Pop culture magic isn't a new concept. One notable influence in the chaos magic scene is the work of H.P. Lovecraft. Though Lovecraft himself didn't intend for his stories to be used by occultists, the Cthulhu Mythos has been adopted as a modern mythos. Lovecraftian concepts have been invoked in rituals, and Cthulhu himself has become an egregore of sorts, fueled and energized by fans and occultists alike.

Similarly, in earlier times, people worked magic through the stories and archetypes of their own time – gods, heroes, saints, and spirits that were part of their collective understanding of reality. Pop culture magic follows in this age-old tradition of using stories, myths, and legends as a source of power.

Invoking pop culture archetypes is one of the most common ways to engage with this practice, but there are many other techniques for incorporating pop culture into magic. One of the most powerful tools is the concept of the hypersigil, which I have already introduced. Hypersigils use narrative as a medium for spell work, and any story, whether from a TV series, book, or video game, can be shaped into a hypersigil to manifest change in the real world.

For instance, role-playing games like *Dungeons & Dragons* allow for the creation of entire characters, worlds, and narratives. When a magician creates a character in a game, they are creating a hypersigil – a narrative avatar through which they can channel magical intention. By aligning their magical goals with the goals of their character, they can blur the lines between the game world and the real world. Just as Grant Morrison accidentally discovered the hypersigil through his work in comics, gamers can craft spells through the stories they play out in these fictional worlds.

Video games offer a great resource for magical inspiration. Many video games feature systems of magic – spells, potions, and rituals – that can be adapted into a real-world practice. For example, in *Skyrim*, spells like "Calm" or "Oakflesh" can inspire the creation of sigils or spells intended to influence our reality in similar ways. Many video games will have a variation of "beast mode", granting characters a surge of power in battle. Imagine how this transformative this could be in your own life – what would your personal "beast mode" look like? Chaos magic, at its core, is a manipulation of belief. Pop culture gives us an endless supply of symbols, ready to be reshaped, invoked, or used as magical tools.

Divination

Entire books have been dedicated to the art of divination. Rather than delving into an exhaustive analysis, I would like to take the opportunity to stress its importance in a chaos magic practice – and why you should find a system of divination that works best for you.

Divination is the practice of using supernatural means to predict the future, gain spiritual wisdom and insight, or to uncover hidden truths. It can be used as a diagnostic tool *prior* to performing rituals and as a tool used *during* rituals to communicate with spirits or assess the progress of the ritual itself.

The art of divination can include working with tarot cards, oracles, runes, dowsing rods, pendulums, spirit boards, scrying, and more. Each of these divination systems offers its own unique perspective and flavor for interpreting the energies playing into our lives.

For example, if a problem arises and you are unsure what to do, you can consult your chosen form of divination to diagnose the problem and find the best-fitting solution. Let's say you happen to intuitively feel you are under a spiritual attack. You are unsure if it is coming from an external source or your own self-fulfilling prophecies. Divination can help you identify if you are, in fact, under spiritual attack, where the attack may be coming from (whether it is external, internal, or both), and what to do moving forward.

Or, let's say you would like to use your chosen system of divination to communicate with spirits during a ritual. You pick up your pendulum or dowsing rods and begin to communicate. You can also use these tools to assess how the ritual is going and as a means of receiving additional messages from the entities you choose to invoke.

Divination can also be used as a window into the psyche and help guide your subconscious belief journaling. Refer back to Exercise 3 where I provided you with journaling prompts to explore with regards to limiting beliefs your subconscious harbors. Sit down with your journal. Pull a tarot card with each prompt. What wisdom can be learned from this particular card as it pertains to the question being asked? This can guide the practitioner into deeper thought.

Among the many forms of divination, scrying is particularly helpful in occult rituals. This technique involves gazing into reflective surfaces – such as crystal balls, black scrying mirrors, pools of water, candle flames, or the smoke from incense – to receive visions or messages from the subconscious mind or spiritual realm. Scrying can take various forms and it involves interpreting the shapes that present themselves. It often requires a great deal of introspection to interpret the symbolism seen – relating it back to one's own psyche and individual interpretation.

Scrying can be seen as one of the most helpful forms of divination because not only does it give you the ability to receive messages in ritual – it also inadvertently forces the practitioner to look within themselves for the answer. Let's say a practitioner has lit a stick of frankincense incense as an offering to a spirit they wish to invoke. During the ritual, while the incense is lit, an image of a bird appears in the billowing smoke. Of course, a practitioner can quickly Google "What is the symbolism of a bird?" However, it is much more powerful to reflect in your own mind what the symbolism means to you in the context of this spirit. Perhaps the spirit you are invoking is associated with birds, further confirming you are working with the right spirit. Or perhaps you have always interpreted birds as a symbol of freedom and flight. How does this pertain to your current life circumstances? What wisdom can you acquire from this message? This is how one develops personal gnosis. With trial and error, assessing various symbols and how they pertain to *your* psyche, you are able to find deeper meaning in messages from the universe. Ultimately, the practice of scrying not only increases the magician's ability to focus and quiet the mind but also creates a deeper connection to the subconscious – allowing for the magician to truly know thyself.

For a chaos magician, divination moves beyond predicting the future. It becomes a method for introspection, exploration, and offers the ability to reshape one's belief systems. By observing and journaling on the symbols, messages, and insights gained from one's chosen system of divination, one can reflect on the inner narratives and repeating patterns that have been conditioned over time.

Personal gnosis, as mentioned many times throughout this book, is heavily emphasized in a chaos magic practice. In the context of divination, it is not just about buying a deck of tarot cards and memorizing what each card traditionally means – according to the little booklet inside the box. It is about assessing symbolism, recognizing patterns, and developing your own wisdom.

In tarot, the Magician card has its own traditional meaning. However, when I encounter the Magician card in a reading, it means something unique to me. I have analyzed patterns in my life when the Magician card presents itself which gives me a personal relationship with this card. When the Magician appears, I know what it is telling me and what I must do. When certain tarot cards show up, my personal relationship with them and my gnosis guides me to better understand their messages in the context of my psyche. Divination then becomes a process of introspection – a mirror held to the deepest parts of your mind.

In short, choose a system of divination, pick up your journal, and begin.

Exercise 10: The Initiation Ritual

No one can initiate you into this practice but yourself. Embrace the idea of full creative freedom and modify this ritual to your liking, infusing it with elements of chaos and play. The purpose of this ritual is to build a sense of confidence within you – you already possess the knowledge needed to begin your magical journey.

Materials:

- Whatever the hell you want.

Procedure:

1. You may have noticed various shapes at the beginning of each chapter. These shapes, built upon each other progressively through each chapter, represent your growth and the knowledge you have acquired in this book. Feel free to use this sigil in your ritual to represent your initiation into chaos magic.

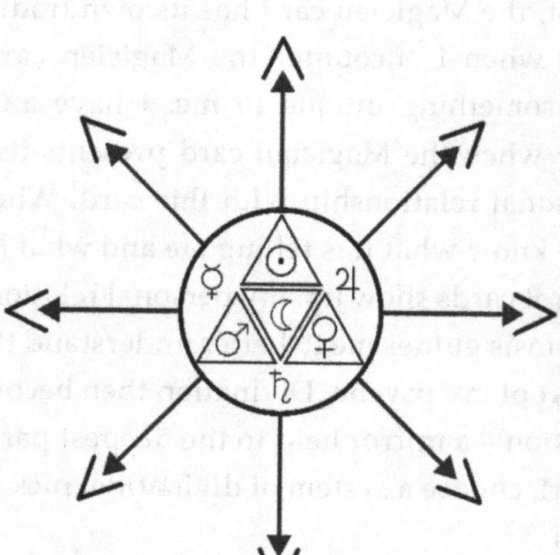

2. Begin by finding a space where you can be undisturbed. Create a circle on the ground, large enough for you to sit in. Draw the sigil on a piece of paper and place it in the center of the circle. You may wish to outline the circle

with items that represent your spiritual practice or items that feel intrinsically *you.*

3. Sit in the center of the circle on top of the sigil. Take a deep breath and ground yourself. Reflect on your journey thus far and articulate your intentions for this initiation. What do you wish to achieve through chaos magic? Write these intentions down in your *Alice.* You may wish to spend some time writing out goals that you and your *Alice* can achieve together.
4. You may choose to perform a mirror meditation. Holding a mirror, gaze into it and reflect upon the person you have been and the person you aspire to become. As you observe your reflection, visualize the limitations of your old self melting away. Speak aloud your old beliefs and fears, and then shatter them by declaring:

   "I am not bound by these limitations! I release you!"

5. You may choose to invoke certain archetypal beings or perform divination.
6. Pick up the sigil. Enter a gnostic state to activate the sigil with your intention. Speak the words:

   "I initiate myself into chaos, welcoming the unknown, and embracing my power."

7. Burn the sigil. Keep the ashes to use in future workings or bury them into the earth.
8. Give thanks to any energies or entities you have brought into the ritual space and release them. Open the circle. You are now officially initiated into your chaos magic practice. *And so it is.*

Recommended Reading

Chapter 1: What Is Chaos Magic?

- *Liber Null & Psychonaut* by Peter J. Carroll
- *Condensed Chaos* by Phil Hine
- *The Book of Results* by Ray Sherwin

Chapter 2: Belief as a Tool

- *The Case Against Reality: Why Evolution Hid the Truth from Our Eyes* by Donald Hoffman

Chapter 3: Deconditioning

- *Prometheus Rising* by Robert Anton Wilson, Forward by Israel Regardie

Chapter 4: Gnosis

- *The Mind Illuminated: A Complete Meditation Guide Integrating Buddhist Wisdom and Brain Science* by John Yates (Culadasa), Matthew Immergut, and Jeremy Graves
- *Psychic Witch: A Metaphysical Guide to Meditation, Magick & Manifestation* by Mat Auryn
- *Llewellyn's Complete Book of Lucid Dreaming* by Clare R. Johnson, PhD

Chapter 5: Sigils & Beyond

- *Practical Sigil Magic* by Frater U.:D.:

- *Practical Planetary Magick* by David Rankine and Sorita d'Este
- *The Book of Pleasure (Self-Love): The Psychology of Ecstasy* by Austin Osman Spare
- *Liber Null* by Peter Carroll
- *Weaving fate: Hypersigils, Changing the Past & Telling True Lies* by Aiden Wachter
- *Visual Magick: A Manual of Freestyle Shamanism* by Jan Fries

Chapter 6: Magical Entities

- *Creating Magickal Entities* by David Michael Cuningham with Contributions by Taylor Ellwood & Amanda R. Wagener
- *Walking With Magical Entities* by Taylor Ellwood
- *Creating Consciousness: The Psychology and Art of Tulpamancy* by Nicholas Guillette
- *Egregores: The Occult Entities That Watch Over Human Destiny* by Mark Stavish

Chapter 7: More Chaos Techniques

The following list of books is meant to further inspire your chaos magic practice. I am not including fictional books that have influenced the chaos magic movement. Inspiration can be found in any fictional story that speaks to the practitioner. Keep in mind that every author on this list presents a slightly different flavor of chaos magic. If you do not resonate with one particular style of writing or practicing, I encourage you to explore other books on this list. This is also, by no means, an exhaustive list.

- *Magick in Theory and Practice* (Liber ABA, Book 4) by Aleister Crowley and everything else
- *SSOTBME Revised: An Essay on Magic* by Ramsey Dukes

- *Liber Kaos* by Peter Carroll and other works by this author
- *Prime Chaos* by Phil Hine and other works by this author
- *Advanced Magick for Beginners* by Alan Chapman
- *Chaotopia! Sorcery and Ecstasy in the Fifth Aeon* by Dave Lee and other works by this author
- *Hands-On Chaos Magic: Reality Manipulation through the Ovayki Current* by Andrieh Vitimus
- *Chaos Magick* by Seth Cardorra
- *Now That's What I Call Chaos Magick* by Julian Vayne and Greg Humphries
- *The Chaos Protocols: Magical Techniques for Navigating the New Economic Reality* by Gordon White
- *This Is Chaos: Embracing the Future of Magic* by Peter Carrol, Ronald Hutton, Aidan Wachter, Carl Abrahamsson, Dave Lee, Ivy Corvus, Jaq D. Hawkins, Jozef Karika, Jacob Sipes, Julian Vayne, Lionel Snell, Mariana Pinzón, Sinobu Kurono, and Sanhre Daffowt
- *Chaonomicon: Quintessential Chaos for the Serious Magician* by Jaq D. Hawkins
- *Rebel Witch: Carve the Craft That's Yours Alone* by Kelly-Ann Maddox
- *Six Ways: Approaches & Entries for Practical Magic* by Aiden Wachter

About the Author

Ivy Corvus is an American occultist who has practiced various occult philosophies for over 15 years. She is best known on YouTube where she has cultivated a reputation as an experimental chaos magician. Through her quickly growing channel, established in 2022, Ivy shares knowledge, conducts interviews with esteemed occult authors and practitioners, and fosters new ideas that represent a new generation within the occult community.

Ivy has always expressed an interest in the intersection of science and spirituality. She is both a healthcare practitioner and an undergraduate student: double-majoring in psychology and molecular biosciences. Her passion lies in understanding the interconnectedness of the universe and guiding others along their spiritual journeys. She lives in the Pacific Northwest with her partner, her animals, and her garden of gnomes.

Bibliography

Amen, D. G. (2009). *The Brain in Love: 12 Lessons to Enhance Your Love Life*. Three Rivers Press.

Auryn, M. (2020). *Psychic Witch: A Metaphysical Guide to Meditation, Magick & Manifestation*. Llewellyn Publications.

Backstein, K. & Mitra, A. (1992). *The Blind Men and the Elephant*. Scholastic Inc.

Boccia, M., Piccardi L., & Guariglia, P. (2015). The meditative mind: A comprehensive meta-analysis of MRI studies. *BioMed Research International, 2015,* 1–11. https://doi.org/10.1155/2015/419808

Cardorra, S. (2012). *Chaos Magick*. CreateSpace.

Carroll, P. J. (1987). *Liber Null & Psychonaut*. Red Wheel Weiser.

Carroll, P. J. (1992). *Liber Kaos*. S. Weiser.

Carroll, P., Hutton, R., Corvus, I., Vayne, J., Hawkins, J. D., Abrahamsson, C., Wachter, A., Daffowt, S., Kurono, S., Pinzon, M., Snell, L., Sipes, J., Karika, J. & Lee, D. (2025). *This is Chaos: Embracing the Future of Magic*. Weiser Books.

Crowley, A., Desti, M. & Waddell, L. (1998). *Magick: Liber Aba*. Murine Press.

Domjan, M. & Grau, J. W. (2020). *The Principles of Learning and Behavior*. Wadsworth.

Dukes, R. (2002). *S.S.O.T.B.M.E. Revised: An Essay on Magic*. The Mouse that Spins.

Evans, R. G. (2006, March). *The blind men, the elephant and the CT Scanner*. Healthcare Policy. https://www.ncbi.nlm.nih.gov/pmc/articles/PMC2585342/

Fortune, D. (2022). *The Mystical Qabalah*. Weiser Books.

Frater, U. :D. (2012). *Practical Sigil Magic: Creating Personal Symbols for Success*. Llewellyn Publications.

Fries, J. (2000). *Visual Magick: A Practical Guide to Trance, Sigils and Visualization Techniques*. Mandrake.

Garcia Gaes, L. (2018). Binaural beats: Brain wave induction and the use of binaural beats to induce brain wave patterns. *Current Research: Integrative Medicine, 03*(02). https://doi.org/10.4172/2529-797x.1000030

Gaur, S., Panjwani, U. & Kumar, B. (2020). EEG Brain Wave Dynamics: A systematic review and meta analysis on effect of yoga on mind relaxation. *Journal of Biomedical Research & Environmental Sciences, 1*(7), 353–362. https://doi.org/10.37871/jbres1166

Guillette, N. (2019). *Creating Consciousness: The Psychology and Art of Tulpamancy*. Independently Published.

Hernández, S. (2022, November 22). *Anil Seth: "Reality is a Controlled Hallucination."* CCCB LAB. https://lab.cccb.org/en/anil-seth-reality-is-a-controlled-hallucination/

Hine, P. & Carroll, P. J. (2010). *Condensed Chaos: An Introduction to Chaos Magic*. Original Falcon Press.

Hine, P. & Morrison, G. (2009). *Prime Chaos: Adventures in Chaos Magic*. Original Falcon Press.

Hoffman, D. D. (2022). *The Case Against Reality: Why Evolution Hid the Truth From Our Eyes*. W.W. Norton & Company, Inc.

Johnson, C. R. (2017). *Llewellyn's Complete book of Lucid Dreaming*. Llewellyn Worldwide, LTD.

Komisaruk, B. R., Beyer, C. & Whipple, B. (2006). *The Science of Orgasm*. Johns Hopkins University Press.

La Vey, A. S. (2017). *The Satanic Bible*. Ishi Press International.

Lee, D. (2009). *Chaotopia!: Sorcery and Ecstasy in the Fifth Aeon*. Mandrake.

Lutz, A., Greischar, L. L., Rawlings, N. B., Ricard, M. & Davidson, R. J. (2004). Long-term meditators self-induce high-amplitude gamma synchrony during mental practice.

Proceedings of the National Academy of Sciences, 101(46), 16369–16373. https://doi.org/10.1073/pnas.0407401101

Morrison, G. (2008). *Grant Morrison – Pop magic*. WordPress. https://doctormcg.files.wordpress.com/2018/02/morrison-pop-magik-pdf.pdf

Rankine, D. & D'Este, S. (2007). *Practical Planetary Magick: Working the Magick of the Classical Planets in the Western Mystery Tradition*. Avalonia.

Seth, P. A. (2022). *Being You: A New Science of Consciousness*. Faber and Faber.

Sherwin, R. (2005). *The Book of Results*. Lulu Enterprises.

Spare, A. O., Pochin, S., Moore, A. & Wallace, W. (2023). *The Book of Pleasure: 1909-1913*. Jerusalem Press.

Stavish, M. (2018). *Egregores: The Occult Entities That Watch Over Human Destiny*. Inner Traditions.

Vitimus, A. (2009). *Hands-On Chaos Magic: Reality Manipulation Through the Ovayki Current*. Llewellyn Publications.

Wachter, A. (2020). *Weaving fate: Hypersigils, Changing the Past & Telling True Lies*. Red Temple Press.

Wilson, R. A. & Regardie, I. (2016). *Prometheus Rising*. New Falcon Publications.

Yates, J., Graves, J. & Immergut, M. (2017). *The Mind Illuminated: A Complete Meditation Guide Integrating Buddhist Wisdom and Brain Science*. Touchstone.

MOON BOOKS
PAGANISM & SHAMANISM

What is Paganism? A religion, a spirituality, an alternative belief system, nature worship? You can find support for all these definitions (and many more) in dictionaries, encyclopaedias, and text books of religion, but subscribe to any one and the truth will evade you. Above all Paganism is a creative pursuit, an encounter with reality, an exploration of meaning and an expression of the soul. Druids, Heathens, Wiccans and others, all contribute their insights and literary riches to the Pagan tradition. Moon Books invites you to begin or to deepen your own encounter, right here, right now.

If you have enjoyed this book, why not tell other readers by posting a review on your preferred book site.

Bestsellers from Moon Books
Pagan Portals Series

The Morrigan

Meeting the Great Queens

Morgan Daimler

Ancient and enigmatic, the Morrigan reaches out to us. On shadowed wings and in raven's call, meet the ancient Irish goddess of war, battle, prophecy, death, sovereignty, and magic.

Paperback: 978-1-78279-833-0 ebook: 978-1-78279-834-7

The Awen Alone

Walking the Path of the Solitary Druid

Joanna van der Hoeven

An introductory guide for the solitary Druid, The Awen Alone will accompany you as you explore, and seek out your own place within the natural world.

Paperback: 978-1-78279-547-6 ebook: 978-1-78279-546-9

Moon Magic

Rachel Patterson

An introduction to working with the phases of the Moon, what they are and how to live in harmony with the lunar year and to utilise all the magical powers it provides.

Paperback: 978-1-78279-281-9 ebook: 978-1-78279-282-6

Hekate

A Devotional

Vivienne Moss

Hekate, Queen of Witches and the Shadow-Lands, haunts the pages of this devotional bringing magic and enchantment into your lives

Paperback: 978-1-78535-161-7 ebook: 978-1-78535-162-4

Bestsellers from Moon Books

Keeping Her Keys
An Introduction to Hekate's Modern Witchcraft
Cyndi Brannen
Blending Hekate, witchcraft and personal development together to create
a powerful new magickal perspective.
Paperback: 978-1-78904-075-3 ebook 978-1-78904-076-0

Journey to the Dark Goddess
How to Return to Your Soul
Jane Meredith
Discover the powerful secrets of the Dark Goddess and transform your depression, grief and pain into healing and integration.
Paperback: 978-1-84694-677-6 ebook: 978-1-78099-223-5

Shamanic Reiki
Expanded Ways of Working with Universal Life Force Energy
Llyn Roberts, Robert Levy
Shamanism and Reiki are each powerful ways of healing; together, their power multiplies. Shamanic Reiki introduces techniques to help healers and Reiki practitioners tap ancient healing wisdom.
Paperback: 978-1-84694-037-8 ebook: 978-1-84694-650-9

Southern Cunning
Folkloric Witchcraft in the American South
Aaron Oberon
Modern witchcraft with a Southern flair, this book is a journey through the folklore of the American South and a look at the power these stories hold for modern witches.
Paperback: 978-1-78904-196-5 ebook: 978-1-78904-197-2

Readers of ebooks can buy or view any of these bestsellers by clicking on the live link in the title. Most titles are published in paperback and as an ebook. Paperbacks are available in traditional bookshops. Both print and ebook formats are available online.

Find more titles and sign up to our readers' newsletter
www.collectiveinkbooks.com/paganism

For video content, author interviews and more, please subscribe to our YouTube channel.

MoonBooksPublishing

Follow us on social media for book news, promotions and more:

Facebook: Moon Books

Instagram: @MoonBooksCI

X: @MoonBooksCI

TikTok: @MoonBooksCI